POLITICS AND THE
ADMINISTRATION OF JUSTICE

The SAGE Series on
POLITICS AND THE LEGAL ORDER

Editor: **Joel B. Grossman,** University of Wisconsin

Volume II, SAGE SERIES ON POLITICS AND THE LEGAL ORDER,
Joel B. Grossman, *Series Editor*

POLITICS AND THE
ADMINISTRATION OF JUSTICE

GEORGE F. COLE
University of Connecticut

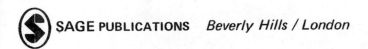 **SAGE PUBLICATIONS** *Beverly Hills / London*

For information address:

SAGE PUBLICATIONS, INC.
275 South Beverly Drive
Beverly Hills, California 90212

SAGE PUBLICATIONS LTD
St George's House / 44 Hatton Garden
London E C 1

Printed in the United States of America

International Standard Book Number 0-8039-0169-0

Library of Congress Catalog Card No. 72-84047

SECOND PRINTING

To My Parents

EDITOR'S FOREWORD

There is today no greater subject of domestic political controversy than the efficacy of the criminal justice system. It is attacked by one side as inept in the capture of criminals and the deterrence of crime. And it is charged by the other with disrespect for constitutional rights; criminal defendants are "processed" rather than adjudicated, and the ideals of due process are compromised in favor of administrative efficiency. One side argues that court decisions setting rules for police behavior "handcuff" the police and contribute to increases in crime. The other side responds that illegal police behavior is a greater threat to our society than ordinary crime and that the courts do not do enough to prevent it. Thus, almost everybody, for different reasons, agrees that the criminal justice system is defective.

In this book Professor Cole seeks to synthesize the burgeoning literature describing the criminal justice system. His premise is that only by understanding the system, and the diverse and often conflicting roles which comprise it, can some intelligent effort be made to correct its deficiencies. He is very persuasive in arguing that the values which dominate the system, and the way its component roles are defined, reflect the broader political culture of the society. He also notes the political and other pressures to which police, prosecutorial, and judicial behavior is often subject. The author utilizes a number of social science approaches, including exchange theory, role theory, and bureaucratic theory. Yet there is little jargon and a complex subject is described in a clear exposition that will benefit scholars but also be readable to the informed layman.

Joel B. Grossman
Madison, Wisconsin
March 1972

ACKNOWLEDGEMENTS

Books are written only with the assistance and stimulation of many people. My debts are many. David Danelski, Alex Gottfried, and John Kessel have provided intellectual models which have been important influences on my growth. Joel Grossman contributed needed comments and suggestions during the manuscript preparation. Special thanks are extended to the editors of the *Law and Society Review* and the *Rutgers-Camden Law Journal* for permission to include published materials. The assistance of Allegheny College and the University of Connecticut Research Foundation is gratefully acknowledged. Betty Seaver's exceptional talents as a writing critic prevented countless errors. Joan, David, and Jonathan continue to provide the love and surprises which make the larger enterprise worthwhile. I hope that the expectations of these many people will be fulfilled.

G.F.C.

Storrs, Connecticut
Summer, 1971

CONTENTS

POLITICS AND THE
ADMINISTRATION OF JUSTICE

POLITICS AND CRIMINAL JUSTICE

"It is well to remember that although the law is abstract, its decision-making institutions deal with a concrete and practical world."[1]

Black militant Lee Otis Johnson is sentenced by a Houston court to thirty years in the penitentiary for giving away one marijuana cigarette;[2] public officials in "Wincanton, U.S.A." allow a gambling syndicate to flourish in return for kickbacks and other favors;[3] party membership is the key variable in allocating judgeships and other legal offices; police agree to keep vagrants on skid row and away from the "better" hotels; felony charges against an influential attorney are dropped; candidates for public office use the issue of "law and order" to gain votes.

Although the relationship between law and politics has been recognized since ancient times, these illustrations serve to reawaken us to the fact that the administration of criminal justice is not the statutory image of justice, in which the rule of law prevails and equal treatment is accorded each individual. Rather, like all legal institutions, the criminal justice system is "political" since it is engaged in the formulation and administration of public policies where choices must be made among such competing values as the rights of defendants, protection of

15

persons and property, justice, and freedom. That various groups in society interpret these values differently is obvious. Decisions result from the influence of the political power of decision makers and the relative strength of competing elites. Judicial personnel are engaged in the "authoritative allocation of values" in the same sense as are other governmental decision makers whose positions are generally perceived as political.[4] As noted by Klonoski and Mendelsohn "political considerations broadly conceived, explain to a large extent 'who gets or does not get—in what amount—and how, the "good" ' (justice) that is hopefully produced by the legal system" in the setting of the local community.[5]

The administration of criminal justice is complicated by the fact that laws are often ambiguous, full enforcement of them is both impossible and undesirable, and many "on the books" no longer have public support. The result is a selective process in which legal actors are given a wide range of discretionary powers to determine who will be arrested, on what charges they will be prosecuted, and the disposition of their cases. Because these decisions are made on a daily basis within the context of the local community, the political ramifications of the system are heightened.

Besides the general pervasiveness of politics in the administration of justice, there are specific ways in which political influences permeate the legal system. It has long been recognized that political parties are a weighty ingredient in the recruitment of judges, prosecutors, and other legal personnel. In many American cities the road to a judgeship is paved with deeds performed for the party. Prosecuting attorneys are also recognized as political actors of consequence. Because of their power of discretion, the fact that they are usually elected with party support, and the patronage which they have at their disposal, prosecutors are pivotal figures with ties to both the internal politics of the justice system and to local political organizations. Likewise, Wilson has shown that the appointment of the police administrator is a key political decision which structures the style of law enforcement a community can expect.[6]

In many ways the administration of criminal justice is a community affairs; political influentials and interest groups work to insure that the law will be applied in ways consistent with their perception of local values. The Chicago "police riot" during the 1968 Democratic national convention, and the Walker Report which followed can be understood only within the context of the political culture of that city and the Daley machine. Kai Erickson's fine study of deviance among the Massachusetts Puritans makes clear the impact of community values on the justice process.[7] During times of stress, he suggests, the labeling of individuals or groups as deviant alerts members to shared values, thus reinforcing the boundaries of the community. Criminal law may not necessarily allocate "justice" in the normative sense, but it does "maintain a level of public order consistent with the preferences of decision makers and their most significant constituencies."[8]

Contemporary evidence of the influence of community norms on the machinery of criminal justice may be found by comparing the disposition of criminal cases in a variety of cities, or by contrasting sentences handed out by judges in small towns with those given in metropolitan areas. What the rural judge may perceive as a "crime wave" is often viewed as routine by his urban counterpart. Since most criminologists believe that the process of labeling activity as criminal is a function of societal norms, the influence of local attitudes is always present. As sociologist Richard Quinney has said,

> "Criminal definitions are applied by the segments of society that have the power to shape the enforcement and administration of criminal law. Crime is political behavior and the criminal becomes in fact a member of a 'minority group' without sufficient public support to dominate the control of the police power of the state."[9]

But it is also important to stress that laws are applied by individuals within the context of local influences. The experience of blacks in the South, union organizers among the agricultural workers of California, and persons called "hippies" attests to the fact that the legal system is used to allocate justice in a manner which conforms to community values and prejudices. Local sheriffs often feel that they have a responsibility to protect the community from those whose attitudes and life style may not conform.

Decentralization is particularly noted when the role of state government in the administration of criminal justice is examined. The laws which are enforced are state laws, but their enforcement is left to a multitude of agencies at the local level which have wide powers of discretion. Attorneys general usually have little authority under the criminal law and can exercise that only under extreme circumstances.[10] In most states there is no unit to coordinate activities among law enforcement officials. Likewise, the independent election or appointment of judges mean that the state appellate courts have little formal authority over the courts of first instance manned by local judges.

It is also at the local level that the individual has contact with the legal process. Although most citizens will not ever appear in court or at the police station, their perception of the quality of justice will greatly affect their willingness to abide by the laws of the community. Robert Kennedy noted that "the poor man looks upon the law as an enemy, not as a friend. For him the law is always taking something away."[11] Thus if it is widely assumed that the police can be bribed, that certain groups are singled out for harsh treatment, or that lawbreaking will not result in punishment of offenders, the political system will lose much of its dominion over the behavior of the affected populace. As Pound once said, criminal law "must safeguard the general security and the individual life against abuse of criminal procedure while at the same time making that procedure as effective as possible for the securing of the whole scheme of social interests."[12] Reports from the President's Commission on Law Enforcement and Administration of Justice indicate that abuses in the criminal justice system have been instrumental in alienating many Americans from the values of the society.

Although there is a tendency to divide the administration of criminal justice into enforcement and adjudication, this distinction neglects the very close interrelationship and overlapping among system actors. Within the justice system, the outputs of one decision-making section, such as the police, become the inputs to another, such as the prosecutor. Likewise, the courts, coroner, grand jury, bondsman, and defense counsel have continuing relationships concerning a wide variety of actions which have an impact on the allocation of justice. The internal politics of the criminal justice bureaucracy immerses officials in a network of interpersonal contacts which emphasizes their interdependence. Each judicial actor has goals and values which are personal and are related to his own job situation. To achieve these goals each needs the cooperation of others. Bargaining among judicial officials over the conditions governing the disposition of each case appears to be typical of decision-making. To view the justice process as a machine in which decisions are made solely on the basis of "rational" criteria, such as evidence, misses the very personal ways in which justice is individualized.

The confluence of law, administration, and politics results in a system in which officials who are sensitive to the political process make decisions at various points concerning the arrest, charges, conviction, and sentences of defendants. The local legal subsystem is very much involved in the allocation of the costs and benefits of the political system. Thus the judicial process induces conditions which are important to the political needs of legal actors. Criminal prosecutions "provide opportunities for the political system to affect judicial decisions and for the judicial process to provide favors which nourish political organizations."[13] For example, both judges and prosecutors must bid for re-election, the courthouse is a base for much patronage, and certain laws may or may not be enforced, depending upon the needs of influentials.

The primary goal of this investigation is to examine the administration of criminal justice within the context of the local political system. Politics includes not only an emphasis on the use of the legal system for partisan gain, but more importantly, serves to focus attention on the processes through which public decisions are made and conflict resolved. The analysis is therefore based on the assumptions that the judicial process is best understood as a subsystem of the larger political system, and that political considerations are a factor in decision-making. Shall charges be filed against powerful gambling interests or shall the resources of law enforcement be directed against the derelicts on skid row? Do defendants with counsel obtain more lenient treatment from the prosecutor's office and the courts than do indigents? How do other agencies of government limit the offices of criminal justice? By focusing upon the political and social linkages among these systems it is expected that decision-making in the administration of criminal justice will be viewed as a principal ingredient in the authoritative allocation of values.

THE CRIMINAL JUSTICE CRISIS

"Law and order" has become one of the most explosive political slogans. At a time when many Americans are faced with a rising crime rate, libertarian decisions by the Supreme Court, racial violence, and urban change, politicians have found that voters are easily aroused by the phrase. This became especially clear during the 1968 presidential campaign when Richard Nixon used the issue of crime as the core of his strategy. By appealing through a simplistic approach to a complex social problem, he elicited tremendous crowd responses, the most vigorous to his almost daily pledge that his first act upon assuming office would be to replace Attorney General Ramsey Clark for "coddling criminals." That criminal law enforcement in this country is primarily a local concern was not mentioned by the candidate nor recognized by the general public.

Like most political slogans, "law and order" is a contraction for a larger number of underlying attitudes which are either too complex or too impolitic to be given utterance. Undoubtedly this attitude cluster is a symbol of racial prejudice for some, a reflection of frustration with societal change for others, and an opportunity for political gain for still others. As Ramsey Clark has written, "The demagogic phrase 'law and order' may mean many things, but to most people today it signifies force, order

trial, rather than upon the local community, where most law enforcement decisions are made. The fact that very few defendants reach the courtroom evidently did not bother social scientists who became enchanted with what Jerome Frank called "the upper court myth":[30] this emphasis on decisions of the Supreme Court probably resulted from the traditional offering of constitutional law in the undergraduate curriculum, as well as the national interest centered on the Court during the era from Hughes to Warren. The emergence of the "behavioral revolution" in the 1950's brought changes in the research interests and methodology of political scientists, but for the most part they continued to study aspects of decision-making by the Supreme Court. This concentration has resulted in the neglect of the judicial process in its entirety.

It has been only during the past decade that a small but growing band of political scientists has discovered the local justice system; this new interest has come at a time when Americans are faced with a rising crime rate, racial violence, and urban change. At the same time there has been a shift of emphasis by the "high court" to consider questions of defendants' rights in the pre-trial phases of the legal process, as shown by the *Miranda* and *Escobedo* decisions. The 1967 Report of the President's Commission on Law Enforcement and Administration of Justice, the formation by Congress of the Law Enforcement Assistance Administration, and the creation of the Law and Society Association have helped to reinvigorate study of the legal system.

Research in the field of criminal justice has been hampered by the fact that there are 52 (state, federal, and District of Columbia) legal systems, no two of which are exactly alike. Each jurisdiction may have a somewhat different emphasis in the political-legal relationship. Because much of the research has been limited to case studies, it is difficult to draw inferences necessary for theory construction. A second problem is the secrecy which surrounds most aspects of the administration of justice. Social science investigators have commented on the reluctance of judicial actors to reveal the secrets of the trade to outsiders. This felt need for secrecy, which sometimes borders on paranoia, is used by judicial actors to shield the process from the public's view. A number of investigators have noted that in this area where vital decisions are being made concerning a defendant's future, the police and prosecutor create the impression that they are uneasy about the way they make decisions and are afraid of the truths being known.[31] Observers have explored the way this aspect of the legal subculture creates bonds which tie the actors together against the supposed enemy—the outsider. The data for empirical studies of the criminal justice process are thus difficult to obtain.

THE ADMINISTRATIVE SYSTEM: AN OVERVIEW

Although the primary focus of social scientists has shifted away from the analysis of the formal structure of institutions, the fact remains that informal arrangements develop in response to the opportunities created by the official blueprint. The criminal justice system operates to apprehend, prosecute, convict, and sentence members of the community who violate the law. However, one is struck by several anomalies which seem to represent the antithesis of such due process values as equal treatment and considered decision-making to which we have been socialized by our ideology.

It is difficult to speak of a criminal justice system in the United States—there are many. As the President's Commission noted, "Every village, town, county, city, and state has its own criminal justice system, and there is a federal one as well. All of them operate somewhat alike. No two of them operate precisely alike."[32] This fact is a result, not only of the community influences discussed above, but also because the federal system and historical influences have given the states freedom to create their own special nuances to basic institutions. Thus discussion of criminal justice is complicated because we must use terms to designate offices which may not fit all circumstances. In the Western states, for example, the prosecuting attorney issues an information to charge a defendant with a felony crime. The older states of the East call the same position "district attorney," and use the common law method of indictment by grand jury.

A second factor which must be recognized is that at all levels the justice process involves a high degree of discretion. Instead of a mechanistic system where law rather than human decisions prevail, it is a process wherein every decision maker—policeman, prosecutor, defense counsel, and judge—may consider a wide variety of elements as he disposes of a case. The need for discretionary power has been justified primarily on two counts: resources and justice. First, it has been pointed out that if every infraction of the law were to be formally processed, the costs would be staggering. Second, there is the belief that in many cases "justice" can be more fully achieved through informal procedures which do not utilize the judiciary. As Matza has said, "Any system promoting individualized justice as a principle . . . must allow this use of discretion."[32] However, such an emphasis raises important questions about the position of the defendant and about the justice which is allocated.

A third feature of the administration of justice is that every part of the system has distinct tasks which are carried out sequentially. Performance must flow efficiently from police to prosecutor to judge. This means that a high degree of interdependence exists; the actions of one part directly affect the work of the others. The courts may deal only with the cases brought to them by the prosecutor, and he, in turn, can deal only with persons arrested by the police. This does not mean that every defendant arrives in the courtroom. On the contrary, a filtering process operates to remove those cases which the relevant actor—policeman, prosecutor, or judge—feels should not be passed on to the next level.

Discretion

One example of the American commitment to the "rule of law" is found on the Department of Justice Building in Washington. Engraved in stone is the phrase, "Where Law Ends, Tyranny Begins." Kenneth Culp Davis has thoughtfully noted that the words are incorrect, since discretion, not tyranny, begins where law ends.[34] In criminal law, where strict adherence to due process values is widely espoused, the presence of broad discretionary powers at all levels of the administration of justice seems a negation of fundamental principles and a threat to personal liberties. Yet there is also the competing emphasis that justice should be individualized, that the "punishment should fit the crime." Discretion may lead to beneficence as well as to tyranny, to justice as well as injustice.

Discretion permeates the administration of criminal justice. From the time that a decision is made to arrest, until sentencing, officials are called upon to make choices in the fulfillment of their responsibilities with very little statutory guidance. Although legislatures are given authority to define criminal conduct, the implementation of their laws is administrative. Criminal law may be viewed as a series of legislatively imposed prohibitions, but the extent to which the law must be acknowledged as a mandate to enforcement agencies is not clear.[35] In addition there is the fact that the definition of criminal conduct and the allocation of enforcement resources require that administrative discretion permeate the system. There are neither the resources nor the desire to enforce the law fully.

The special elements of each case are also grounds for the use of discretion since society maintains the belief that justice should be individualized. This is particularly true when the accused's social and personal characteristics differentiate him from other offenders. Youth, occupation, mental capacity, or race may be used as mitigating aspects which allow for discretion. Although individualized treatment at the sentencing stage is well recognized, these same circumstances appear at earlier points in the justice process, with the result that the police and prosecutor do not always invoke the formal stipulations of the law.

Discretion may be understood as the authority to "act in certain conditions or situations in accordance with an official's . . . own considered judgment and conscience."[36] According to Freund, it allows for the determination in a case on the basis of "considerations not entirely susceptible to proof or disproof."[37] This formulation emphasizes the indefiniteness of legal standards as the basis for discretionary power. Further, it recognizes the technical problems that the legislature has in providing suitable guidance for the administrator. Freund's views have served as the dominant theme in the field of public administration in attempts to increase the definiteness of these standards through formal means: statutes and administrative rules.

Objections to the use of discretion in the administration of justice are primarily leveled at its exercise by the police and prosecutor, less often against the courts or post-sentence agencies. Not only are the police and prosecutors more apparent in their displacement of the rule of law, but the judicial myth helps to insulate the discretionary acts of the courts from public criticism. Hall typifies this attitude when he says, "Police are bound by law to arrest those who they suspect have committed a crime. The question of guilt is a judicial one."[38]

That discretion permeates the administration of justice is obvious. Not only are the policies of local justice influenced by system-wide decisions made by key political and judicial actors, but the daily decisions of individuals in their relationships with the public are made on a discretionary basis. This is especially true regarding policies of selective enforcement and the handling of cooperative informers and accomplices. Prostitution may be allowed if it is confined to certain areas. The police are often urged by business groups to "clean up" sections where the presence of vagrants is thought to deter tourists or shoppers. The prosecutor has the power to decide if he will bring charges, and once instituted, if he will drop them through the simple use of *nolle pros.*, announcement that prosecution has been withdrawn. In addition, he has tremendous leeway as to the type and number of charges which will be lodged against an individual and whether to accept a plea of guilty in exchange for a reduction in the charges. The court has discretion to determine which counts to submit to the jury, within limits the kind of charge to give the jury, and the sentence to be imposed. And so it goes, from the foot patrolman who lectures a juvenile rather than instituting formal proceedings, to the governor who pardons the convicted. Each law enforcement actor has a range of powers which he may use, often without the formal scrutiny of higher officials.

Discretion is exercised in practically every type of social organization. The scope of the powers accorded each position is determined to a large degree by the number and importance of premises which are specified. Thus Simon contends that if only factual premises are left to the subordinate's discretion, the leeway for personal decisions is quite narrow. Alternatively, if the value premises are left to the subordinate's discretion, the "correctness" of his decision "will depend upon the value premises he selects, and there is no universally accepted criterion of right or wrong which can be applied to his selection."[39]

In the administration of justice discretion is exercised with a unique twist. As in few other organizations, discretion in law enforcement and judicial agencies increases as one moves *down* the administrative hierarchy. In most organizations one usually finds that the lowest-ranking members perform the most routinized tasks under supervision, with various mechanisms of quality control employed to check their work.

> "Discretionary jobs are usually arranged sequentially in career patterns so that those requiring larger amounts of discretion are filled after individuals have shown capacity to handle smaller amounts. Many discretionary jobs, moreover, require formal education or training which discourages or weeds out those most allergic to discretion."[40]

With the police, prosecutors, and lower-court judges, however, discretion is exercised most frequently by those who are newest to the organization, who maintain the primary organizational contact with the public, and whose work is usually shielded from the view of supervisors or outside observers.

The patrolman, the lowest-ranking police officer, has the greatest discretion and "thus his behavior presents the greatest concern to police administrators."[41] Working alone or as one of a pair, a patrolman is not under the eye of his supervisor and cannot let the client (suspected criminal) be the sole judge of his failure to invoke enforcement powers. In addition, as Wilson notes, the patrolman, in contrast to the detective, handles matters about which there are apt to be great differences of opinion among the public.[42]

In many prosecution offices, one finds that the deputies are able to decide which cases to accept from the police and the charges to be made. This is done without the control or guidance of the prosecutor. Such a practice may lead to "shopping" by the police to find a deputy who, on the basis of past experience, is most likely to agree to the police recommendation. The potential for policy inconsistency is obvious.

Likewise, the position of lower-court judge lends itself to a very great use of discretion without the dominating influence of higher courts. The justice of the peace and judge of a minor criminal court often operate within an informal context and are able to effectuate justice without necessarily resorting to the strict letter of the law. Again, these positions are staffed by some of the newer members of the bench and those who have not been promoted. They are able to make decisions without the public attention often focused on their brothers farther up the ladder.

In the process of judicial administration a variety of decision makers are able to interpret policy guidelines consistent with their own values and the internal politics of the organization. As noted earlier, decisions which serve to affect the disposition of cases are made at every point. The persons occupying these positions have the ability and power to decide the fate of criminal defendants without adhering strictly to the law. There are circumstances, however, when the political and organizational context of decision-making may limit discretion. Uncertainty about the outcome of a case and the perspective of the "others" in the exchange relationship may inhibit a judicial actor. Public interest may also influence decision makers to adhere closely to the formal rules.

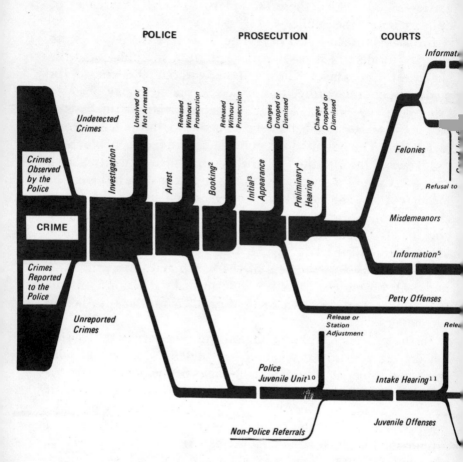

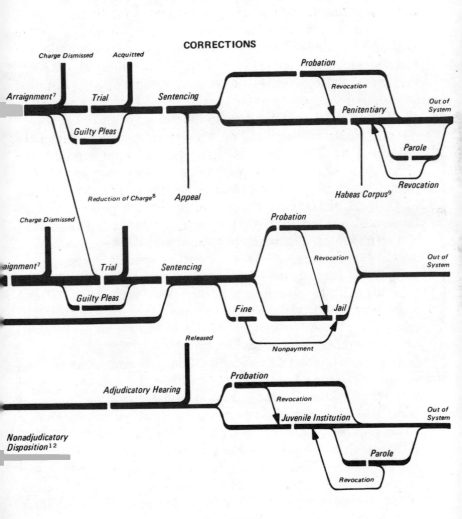

CORRECTIONS

Figure I-1.

The Flow of Decision-Making

Herbert Jacob correctly observes that "the disposition of criminal cases is a long process fraught with detours."[43] Figure I-1 is a general sketch of the criminal justice system prepared by the President's Commission. It shows not only the various processes and actors involved in judicial decision-making, but also indicates the relative volume of cases disposed at various points in the system. The figure should be viewed as an illustration of only the formal dimensions of the process.

The popular conception of the criminal justice machinery supported by a due process ideology and reinforced by the "Perry Mason" image of an adversary system oversimplifies in some respects and overcomplicates in others. The theory holds to an ideal of law enforcement in which the police arrest all those who have committed infractions of the law. The accused is taken before a magistrate who admits him to bail. The prosecutor charges the offender with a specific crime after a preliminary hearing. In the courtroom a "fight," supervised by the judge, is staged between adversaries—defense counsel and prosecutor—so that the truth becomes known. A jury determines the guilt or innocence of the defendant. If he is found guilty, the judge pronounces sentence.

This conception makes some fundamental assumptions which do not correspond to reality. The rational or due process model fails to take note of the many informal arrangements which occur through negotiations among the principal actors. Only a small number of cases ever reach the trial stage. Rather, decisions are made early in the process so that cases which will not result in conviction are filtered out by the police and prosecutor. In addition, in some jurisdictions up to 90 percent of the defendants plead guilty, thus obviating the need for a trial.

Although we may hold to the ideal of full enforcement in which it is assumed that resources will be allocated so that all criminal acts are discovered and all offenders caught, this does not occur. As Figure I-1 indicates, only a small portion of the crimes observed and reported brings forth investigation followed by arrest. Studies have repeatedly shown that offenses are committed by law-abiding citizens far in excess of the number known to the police. As Thurman Arnold pointed out a number of years ago, law enforcement is a twofold problem of keeping order and dramatizing the moral notions of the community. The police and prosecutor determine a policy of law enforcement with the object of using law as "an arsenal of weapons with which to incarcerate certain dangerous individuals who are bothering society."[44] The result is that we assume that resources should be employed to minimize the amount of crime rather than to eliminate it.

During periods of low community tension the public appears to be little concerned about the process. Criminal justice is an individual affair so that only those persons with direct contact understand the work of the police and prosecutors.

> "So long as the vagrants are kept off the streets, the burglars away from the financial district, commercialized vice and organized racketeering away from the middle class suburbs and the occasional spectacular case is somehow 'cracked,' the community does not seriously object to inefficiency and even graft in the lower echelons of officialdom . . . at least as these things are not brought so closely to the community's attention as to be disturbing."[45]

Under these circumstances there is a tendency for officials to accommodate the preferences of the community and pressures of interest groups in the formation of law enforcement policy.

The type of enforcement policy and the allocation of police resources in support of it will determine the amount and kind of criminality discovered. Since the public is unable or unwilling to allow a policy of full enforcement, which would be intolerable and require enormous resources, decisions must be made to distribute the police to various parts of the city. A self-fulfilling prophecy results in which sections of the city perceived as "high crime areas" will be allotted additional patrolmen, with the consequence that more crimes will be discovered, indicating a need for increased surveillance. An independent study might reveal that any area inundated with policemen will show a correspondingly high crime rate.[46]

Preliminary Hearing.—Even after a suspect has been arrested it is necessary to evaluate the evidence and the probability of conviction before deciding to prosecute. In some cases, especially those involving morals violations, there may be no victim or the victim may be unwilling to cooperate in the prosecution. Often the victim swears out a complaint, only to have second thoughts about the necessity of a courtroom recitation of the facts. Sometimes the parents of victims will refuse to cooperate with the prosecutor rather than force their child to relive the emotionally distressing events of the case on the witness stand.

Theoretically, the judicial function of the preliminary hearing is to determine if there is sufficient evidence to hold a person for arraignment on formal charges. From a practical viewpoint, the prosecutor seldom has difficulty in making a prima facie case. Instead, he may use the preliminary hearing to test the value of the evidence and the reliability of witnesses. As a deputy prosecutor told the author, "Generally we send every case up for a preliminary hearing just to see if there is anything there." The hearing is important to prosecutor and defense counsel alike since it affords each an opportunity to view partially the cards held by the other. During the preliminary hearing the prosecutor may decide that the possibility of conviction is low and that his efforts may be more effectively used elsewhere. Likewise, defense counsel may see that his client does not have much of a case, and thus he may be more willing to seek a negotiated plea.

Information or Indictment.—In the United States a person must be formally accused through either an indictment or an information before he may be required to stand trial on a felony criminal charge; the stated legal purpose is to make a preliminary finding that there is sufficient evidence to warrant further action by the state. The major difference between these procedures is that an information may be filed by the prosecutor, while an indictment needs the concurrence of a grand jury. The use of one form rather than the other is related in part to the historical development of various regions. The grand jury never gained a foothold in either Louisiana or California because of the influence of French or Spanish procedures. This, in turn, led to the use of the information throughout most of the states west of the Mississippi River, while the indictment persists only in the eastern states.[47]

The grand jury originated in England as a device to extract "from the people of a locality knowledge concerning matters of interest to the crown."[48] Gradually, however, it became an instrument for the protection of the people against arbitrary accusation by the crown. As the grand jury evolved it made two significant changes in the legal process. First, it cut down on the number of baseless allegations presented to judges. Second, it allowed a degree of local control of prosecution.

Indictment through grand jury action has been criticized as costly and wasteful, yet the institution survives in about half the states and the federal courts as the sole means of bringing charges against the accused. Social scientists have questioned the independence of the grand jury. Lemert reports that both judges and prosecutors conceive grand juries as "extensions of the court system rather than as autonomous agencies of control."[49]

The prosecutor is able to develop a unique relationship with the grand jury through his expert knowledge. The lay members of the jury are dependent upon him for the definition of legal terms and instructions concerning their function. Prosecutors will often assign personable young deputies to the task of advising members of juries and initiating them into the fascinating business of law and crime control. As the Chicago Jury Project revealed, impact on jury deliberations is directly related to the status of the members and the recognition of their competence.[50] It is not surprising that a relationship may develop marked by the prestige and influence of the prosecutor on one hand and the inexperienced laymen on the other. The "assembly-line" aspects of the judicial process usually result in waiver of the right to a grand jury in approximately 80 percent of the cases. In the remainder, the prosecutor is usually able to secure the indictment that he desires. Coates has shown that in Montgomery County (Philadelphia Metropolitan Area), Pennsylvania, indictments resulted in 95 percent of such cases.[51] To the extent that the prosecutor is able to lead the members of the jury to feel that they are participating in the war against crime, he will be successful in securing the indictments desired.

From the defendant's vantage point the information, with its requirement of a preliminary hearing, may have advantages over the indictment. The accused has a right to appear before the examining magistrate with counsel, he may cross-examine witnesses, and produce his own witnesses, considerations not allowed before a grand jury. At the preliminary hearing it is possible for counsel to see the prosecutor's evidence against his client. With this knowledge, counsel is in a better position to structure plea negotiations.

Courtroom.—A visit to a lower criminal court in a metropolitan area would be an educational experience for most Americans. They would see conditions of noise and confusion which stand in dramatic contrast to the dignified and precise judicial machinery one might expect. The courtroom is often a cavernous space, crowded with lawyers, relatives, and defendants, presided over by a judge sitting at one end going through a procedure which is audible only to those directly in front of the bench. Especially in misdemeanor cases there is an informality and speed which is startling to the observer and must be bewildering to the defendant. The President's Commission found that:

> "speed is the watchword. Trials in misdemeanor cases may be over in a matter of 5, 10, or 15 minutes; they rarely last an hour even in relatively complicated cases. Traditional safeguards honored in felony cases lose their meaning in such proceedings; there is still the possibility of lengthy imprisonment or heavy fine."[52]

With some variation throughout the nation a defendant is brought before a judge soon after his arrest to be advised of the charges against him and his constitutional rights. This may be followed by a preliminary hearing, arraignment, and trial.

In fact, very few defendants carry their case to the trial stage; rather a plea of guilty is entered in exchange for a reduction in the charge. Imposition of sentence follows. As Boston Judge Henry T. Lummus has stated, "A criminal court can operate only by inducing the great mass of actually guilty defendants to plead guilty, paying in leniency the price for the plea."[53] Not only are guilty pleas needed because of the heavy caseload, but it is often in the interests of the prosecutor, defendant, and counsel to work out, through negotiations, a method to dispose of the case. The defendant gets a lesser sentence, the prosecutor does not have to spend resources to gather evidence and witnesses, and defense counsel does not have to spend time preparing a defense for which he will receive little compensation.

For the relatively small percentage of defendants who receive a trial, the process (in felony cases) is complicated by the time-consuming and expensive procedure of empaneling a jury, hearing testimony, and obtaining a decision. The trials which come to public attention, such as those of Jack Ruby, Charles Manson, and Bobby Seale, are rare.

Following conviction a decision must be made concerning the sanction to be imposed. Although judges assign the sentence, other decision makers take part; thus many of the organizational considerations influencing the police and prosecutor operate here as well. In many states a pre-sentence investigation is required to give the judge information on the defendant which will aid in his individualization of the justice to be allocated. Although criminal codes place limitations on the sentences which may be imposed, leeway remains for the judge to consider a number of alternatives: suspension, probation, prison, or fine. Social scientists have noted the variety of sentences handed out by judges in the same jurisdiction for similar violations. The influence of such extralegal factors as the background and attitudes of the judge, local norms, administrative pressures, and the defendant's characteristics appear to be the important variables. This often results in the selection of certain defendants, usually the poor, for more severe treatment.

BAIL: AN EXAMPLE OF LAW, POLITICS, AND ADMINISTRATION

The practice of allowing defendants to be released pending their court appearance is a particularly revealing example of the conjunctions between law, politics, and administration. Although the Eighth Amendment prohibits excessive bail, and most state statutes are written so that the system will be administered in a non-discriminatory manner, discretion is accorded to judicial personnel so that they have a great deal of choice in determining the conditions for a defendant's release. Typically this means that individuals with certain characteristics of race, economic status, or life style are required to post a higher bond than do those conforming to community norms. The political implications of the conditions surrounding the granting of bail often exert an influence on decision makers. Within the judicial bureaucracy, bargaining may occur between actors; accordingly, the granting of bail, and the amount, may be viewed as outputs of these transactions.

The practice of allowing defendants to be released from jail pending trial originated in Anglo-Saxon law. In a period when the time between arrest and trial was lengthy and the cost of detention burdensome, bail was used as a convenience to the sheriff in order that he could release prisoners from his responsibility, yet be fairly certain that they would appear in court at the appointed time.[54] Like the modern practice, some form of surety was required, to be forfeited if the accused did not show up as promised. This concept was transferred across the Atlantic with modifications, so that now the right to bail is guaranteed in the federal and most state courts for all but capital cases; excessive bail is prohibited by the Eighth Amendment.

Ideally, the purpose of bail is the same as in older times—to guarantee the presence in court of the defendant. That is the sole legally stated purpose upon which decisions concerning bail are to be made in the United States.[55] Along with our assumption that the accused is innocent until proved guilty, the belief exists that he should not suffer hardships awaiting trial. Bail should not be used as punishment, for the accused has not been found guilty. Rather, he should be allowed to live with his family, to maintain community ties, and to prepare his defense. The amount of bail to be posted should therefore not be based only on the seriousness of the crime, but should consider the suspect's entire personal and social situation as it bears on the likelihood of his appearance.

The reality of the bail system is a long way from the ideal. In almost all jurisdictions the amount of bail is based primarily on the judge's perception of the seriousness of the crime and the record of the accused. In part this results from his lack of information about the accused. Since bail must be allowed within 24-48 hours after an arrest, there is not time to seek out background information upon which to make a more just bail determination.

As shown in Table I-1, crimes against property generally occasion higher bail than do sex offenses or assault, which are crimes against persons. Judges have developed standard rates which are used in both the courtroom and stationhouse to gain the release of prisoners; so many dollars for such and such an offense. Judges often give the police a "bail schedule" which authorizes release of designated categories of offenders who are able to post a specific amount of bail. Since he has full discretion, a judge may set high bail in response to the desires of the police to keep a defendant in custody. Defense attorneys have reported that a bond of any size has the effect of scaring the defendant, but that a high bail implies that the judge believes the crime was vicious or that the defendant might not make the court appearance.[56] Little or no attempt is really

TABLE I-1

BAIL AMOUNTS BY CHARGE, NEW YORK CITY, 1960 (in percentages)

	Bail			
Charges	Under $1500	$1500-$2500	Over $3000	Total %
Assault	51	33	16	100
Burglary	28	46	26	100
Forgery	64	28	8	100
Larceny	59	31	10	100
Narcotics	29	44	27	100
Robbery	12	26	62	100
Sex	62	21	17	100
All cases	40	33	27	100

SOURCE: Ares, Rankin, and Sturz, "Administration of Bail in New York," New York University Law Review, 38 (1963): 79.

made to consider the personal characteristics of the defendant and to assess the probability that he will appear for trial. As the President's Commission has said:

"The persistence of money bail can be explained not by its stated purpose but by the belief of police, prosecutors and courts that the best way to keep a defendant from committing more crimes before trial is to set bail so high that he cannot obtain his release."[57]

Ronald Goldfarb, whose book *Ransom* is a critique of the system, has shown that the emphasis upon monetary bail operates to penalize the poor and to punish in advance of trial those whom society does not like.[58] As shown above, the amount of bail and the number and type of charges are set at the discretion of judicial actors. Bail is often used by the police to punish through confinement when they do not have the evidence to convict. In Des Moines such a device was used against those suspected of operating a motor vehicle while intoxicated (OMVI). Captain Wendell Nichols told reporter Howard James:

"The boys figured the defendant would at least be rapped for the bond [defendants pay a bail bondsman $25 to write a $300 bond for OMVI] and also spend a night in jail."[59]

To post bail a prisoner is required to give the court some form of monetary surety (usually cash), property, or a bond from a bonding company. On some occasions persons who are highly placed in the community are released on their own recognizance, but such actions are rare for all but the most petty of misdemeanors. The effect of the system on the poor is shown by the fact that in New York where the bond fee is only 5 percent, 25 percent of the defendants were unable to raise even the $25 required to furnish $500 bail. At the same time the wealthy businessman and the professional criminal have no difficulty. In some metropolitan night courts one may see lawyers for syndicate-connected prostitutes concluding with fistful of money the arrangements to insure that their clients are quickly released and back on the job.

The inequity of the system is further shown by the fact that those who cannot make bail must remain in jail, where they are treated in the same manner as are convicted prisoners. In a city such as New York, where the median delay between arraignment and trial is 32 days, this can have a disastrous effect on both the defendant and his family. Not only is this an infringement on freedom, but the accused almost always loses his job and family relationships are jeopardized. After such a period in jail, almost half the persons held in lieu of bail in Philadelphia were released after trial either through acquittal, suspended sentence, or probation.[60] It should be noted, however, that judges commonly give suspended sentences to the guilty because of the time passed awaiting trial.

A central figure in the bail system is the professional bondsman, whose services are both visible and available on a 24-hour basis to those defendants who need to produce sufficient cash to secure release.[61] Using either his own assets or those of an insurance company, the bondsman will provide the surety required for a fee of between 5 and 10 percent. Although licensed by the states, the bondsman still has the power to decide for whom he will act as surety and is able to set his own collateral requirements. In addition he may track down and return bail jumpers without extradition and with violent force if necessary.

Like other actors who have an interest in the judicial system, the bondsman exerts a strong influence through his ability to cooperate with the police in exchange for recommendations by jailers or sheriffs of his services rather than those of another bondsman. In return he may refuse to provide bail for defendants whom the police do not wish to see released. Civil rights workers and peace activists have often found that this relationship meant that they had to remain in confinement. Alternatively, McIntyre found several Detroit judges who purposely set low bails because they did not like to see the professional bondsmen making so much money. In January, 1957, $290,000 in bonds was written in Detroit's Recorder's Court. At 10 percent, this resulted in fees of $29,000 split among six or seven bondsmen. One judge commented, "This money should be spent on supporting families and paying attorney's fees rather than filling the bondsman's till."[62]

Attempts at Reform

The Vera Institute of Justice in New York City has been the most active group seeking to reform the bail system.[63] From 1961 to 1964 it carried out a pre-trial parole experiment to determine the number of defendants who could be released on their own recognizance pending trial. This was based on the assumption that courts would grant release if they were given verified information about a defendant's reliability and roots in the community. Vera employees interviewed prisoners soon after their arrest. With the answers to a few questions concerning his job, family, prior criminal record, and associations, a determination was made to ascertain if the accused should be recommended for release. During the first three years of the project over 10,000 defendants were interviewed and approximately 3,500 released due to Vera's work. Only 1.5 percent failed to appear in court at the appointed time. This is almost three times as good a rate as those being released on bail.[64]

In 1964 the Probation Department of the City of New York assumed responsibility for this project and has had comparable success. Based on the attention it has received, similar pre-trail parole projects have been started in over one hundred cities. In Illinois a defendant is allowed to post bond with the court which is returned upon his appearance, thus removing the bondsman. In California, Michigan, and Washington the summons, rather than arrest, is being increasingly used to notify defendants to appear in court. Not only is it important for the defendant and his family that he be free while awaiting trial, but it costs about $7 a day to hold a man in jail. In addition, the Vera program discovered that defendants who were in jail from arrest to trial received unfavorable dispositions much more often than those who were free on bail.[65]

Reform of a different character is present in current suggestions that so-called "preventive detention" should be allowed. Under such schemes a judge could deny bail and require certain defendants to remain in jail pending trial if he felt there was reason to believe they would commit additional crimes in the interim. Civil libertarians have pointed to the threat which such proposals make to basic constitutional values, especially the Sixth and Eighth Amendments, dealing with the right to a speedy trial and prohibitions against excessive bail. In a speech before the Senate in May, 1970, Senator Ervin pointed out that a study conducted by the Justice Department showed that only 5 percent of those arrested for a violent or dangerous crime were rearrested for a similar crime while out on bail. As he demonstrated, passage of the District of Columbia Crime Control Act of 1970 with its preventive detention provisions would mean that nineteen nondangerous persons would be held in order to detain one dangerous defendant! [66]

PLAN OF THE BOOK

This book is designed to integrate materials on the administration of criminal justice which have become available to scholars during the past few years. With a bargaining rather than an adversary model as a basic assumption, the study emphasizes the connections among law, politics, and administration. The idea of bargain justice assumes that decisions are made not as a result of the clash of evidence before the court, but rather through accommodations between the defense and prosecution. By dividing the book into chapters which focus on the activity of each subsection of criminal justice, linkages among the principal actors are examined. These interactions are analyzed as exchange relationships so that the decisions which are made concerning the disposition of cases result from bargains made or implied among participants.

A second characteristic of the book is that each chapter emphasizes a portion of the activity of that subsystem. Thus discretion serves as the focal concept for analysis of the police, decision-making for the prosecutor, bargaining for consideration of the role of defense attorneys, and sentencing as the theme for the chapter on the courts. These emphases reflect the thrust of the scholarship which is available on each aspect of the process.

Chapter IV is a case study based on data collected by the

author in the Office of Prosecuting Attorney of King County (Seattle), Washington. It is a much closer analysis of one criminal justice system than are the other chapters. It is hoped that the reader will understand the transition to the detailed descriptions in this portion of the book.

The American criminal justice system is under pressure to meet the needs of preserving order while protecting the rights of citizens. Faced with an increasingly urbanized and technological society, the "law explosion," and a new awareness on the part of defendants of their constitutional rights, the system must adapt to these new realities. As Attorney General Ramsey Clark has asserted:

"For the system of criminal justice to succeed, it must understand its role and adhere to that role with absolute fidelity. Police, prosecutors, judges and correctional workers must respect the limits of their proper function, avoiding conduct in excess of their authority while fully performing their duty."[67]

NOTES

1. Philip Selznick, "The Sociology of Law," Sociology Today, ed. Robert Merton, Leonard Broom, and Leonard S. Cottrell, Jr. (New York: Basic Books, 1959), 11.

2. Calvin Trillin, "U.S. Journal: Houston," The New Yorker, December 12, 1970, 164.

3. U.S., President, Commission on Law Enforcement and Administration of Justice, Task Force Report: Organized Crime (1967).

4. David Easton, The Political System (New York: Knopf, 1953), esp. 126-141. This is one of the most widely used definitions of politics.

5. James R. Klonoski and Robert I. Mendelsohn, "The Allocation of Justice: A Political Analysis," Journal of Politics, 54 (1965), 323-342.

6. James Q. Wilson, Varieties of Police Behavior (Cambridge: Harvard University Press, 1968), 227.

7. Kai Erickson, Wayward Puritans (New York: John Wiley, 1968).

8. Matthew Holden, Jr., "Politics, Public Order, and Pluralism," The Politics of Local Justice, ed. James R. Klonoski and Robert Mendelsohn (Boston: Little, Brown, 1970), 238.

9. Richard Quinney, The Social Reality of Crime (Boston: Little, Brown, 1970), 18.

10. Morris Ploscowe, "The Significance of Recent Investigations for the Criminal Law and Administration of Criminal Justice," University of Pennsylvania Law Review, 100 (1952), 823.

11. Quoted in *The Politics of Local Justice,* ed. Klonoski and Mendelsohn, xxi.

12. Roscoe Pound, *Criminal Justice in America* (New York: Holt, 1930), 11.

13. Herbert Jacob and Kenneth Vines, "The Role of the Judiciary in American State Politics," *Judicial Decision-Making,* ed. Glendon Schubert (New York: Free Press, 1963), 250.

14. Ramsey Clark, *Crime in America* (New York: Simon and Schuster, 1970), 43.

15. Fred P. Graham, *The Self-Inflicted Wound* (New York: Macmillan, 1970), 12.

16. U.S., Department of Justice, *Uniform Crime Reports,* 1970, 3.

17. New York Times, February 28, 1968, 29.

18. James Q. Wilson, "Crime in the Streets," The Public Interest, Fall, 1966, 26-35.

19. Daniel Bell, "The Myth of Crime Waves," *The End of Ideology,* ed. Daniel Bell (New York: Collier Books, 1961), 151-172.

20. U.S., Department of Justice, *Uniform Crime Reports,* 1970, 5.

21. Wilson, "Crime in the Streets," 29.

22. U.S., President, National Commission on the Causes and Prevention of Violence, *To Establish Domestic Tranquility,* 1969, 18.

23. *The Courts, The Public and the Law Explosion,* ed. Harry W. Jones (Englewood Cliffs: Prentice Hall, 1965), 2.

24. Sanford H. Kadish, "The Crisis of Overcriminalization," Annals, November, 1967, 157-170.

25. Norval Morris and Gordon Hawkins, *The Honest Politician's Guide to Crime Control* (Chicago: University of Chicago Press, 1970), 6.

26. Roscoe Pound, "The Causes of Popular Dissatisfaction with the Administration of Justice," American Bar Association Report, 29 (1906), 395.

27. Edward L. Barrett, Jr., "Criminal Justice: The Problem of Mass Production," *The Courts, The Public and the Law Explosion,* ed. Jones 87.

28. New York Times, January 7, 1971, 1.

29. Warren E. Burger, "State of the Federal Judiciary," address before the American Bar Association, August 10, 1970.

30. Jerome Frank, *Courts on Trial* (New York: Atheneum, 1963), 222.

31. See: William A. Westley, *Violence and the Police* (Cambridge: M.I.T. Press, 1970), 48.

32. U.S., President, Commission on Law Enforcement and Administration of Justice, *The Challenge of Crime in a Free Society,* 1967, 7.

33. David Matza, *Delinquency and Drift* (New York: Wiley, 1964), Ill.

34. Kenneth Culp Davis, *Discretionary Justice* (Baton Rouge: Louisiana State University Press, 1969), 1.

35. Wayne R. LaFave, "The Police and Nonenforcement of the Law—Part I," Wisconsin Law Review, 1962 (January, 1962), 106.

36. Roscoe Pound, "Discretion, Dispensation and Mitigation: The Problems of the Individual Special Case," New York University Law Review, 35 (1960), 925.

37. Ernst Freund, *Administrative Powers over Persons and Property* (Chicago): University of Chicago Press, 1928), 71.

38. Jerome Hall, "Police and Law in a Democratic Society," Indiana Law Journal, 28 (1953), 155.

39. Herbert A. Simon, "Decision-Making and Administrative Organization," Public Administration Review, 4 (1944), 16-25.

40. James D. Thompson, *Organizations in Action* (New York: McGraw-Hill, 1967), 118.

41. Wilson, *Varieties of Police Behavior,* 8.

42. Ibid.

43. Herbert Jacob, *Justice in America* (Boston: Little, Brown, 1965), 149.

44. Arnold, "Law Enforcement—An Attempt at Social Dissection," Yale Law Journal, 42 (November, 1932), 24.

45. *Crime and the Legal Process,* ed. William J. Chambliss (New York: McGraw-Hill, 1969), 99.

46. George Dession, "The Technique of Public Order: Evolving Concepts of Criminal Law," Buffalo Law Review, 5 (1955), 36.

47. Martin Mayers, *The American Legal System* (New York: Harper and Row, 1964), 89.

48. H. L. McClintock, "Indictment by Grand Jury," Minnesota Law Review, 26 (1942), 153-176.

49. Edwin M. Lemert, "The Grand Jury As an Agency of Social Control," American Sociological Review, 10 (December, 1945), 753.

50. Fred L. Strodtbeck, Rita M. James, and Charles Hawkins, "Social Status in Jury Deliberations," American Sociological Review, 22 (December, 1957), 713-719.

51. Walton Coates, "Grand Jury, the Prosecutor's Puppet. Wasteful Nonsense of Criminal Jurisprudence," Pennsylvania Bar Association Quarterly, 33 (March, 1962), 311.

52. President's Commission, *Task Force Report: The Courts, 30.*

53. Donald Newman, *Conviction: The Determination of Guilt or Innocence without Trial* (Boston: Little, Brown, 1966), 62.

54. "Bail: An Ancient Practice Reexamined," Yale Law Journal, 70 (1961), 966-977.

55. President's Commission, *The Challenge of Crime in a Free Society,* 10.

56. *Law Enforcement in the Metropolis,* ed. Donald M. McIntyre (Chicago: American Bar Foundation, 1967), 120.

57. President's Commission, *The Challenge of Crime in a Free Society,* 10.

58. Ronald Goldfarb, *Ransom* (New York: Harper and Row, 1965).

59. Howard James, *Crisis in the Courts* (New York: McKay, 1968), 113.

60. Charles E. Ares, Anne Rankin, and Herbert Sturz, "The Manhattan Bail Project: An Interim Report on the Use of Pre-Trial Parole," New York University Law Review, 38 (1963), 67-92.

61. Caleb Foote, "Compelling Appearance in Court: Administration of Bail in Philadelphia," University of Pennsylvania Law Review, 102 (1954), 1031.

62. *Law Enforcement in the Metropolis,* ed. McIntyre, 122.

63. Ares, Rankin, and Sturz, 67.

64. Goldfarb, 157.

65. Anne Rankin, "The Effect of Pretrial Detention," New York University Law Review, 39 (1964), 641.

66. Congressional Quarterly, *Crime and the Law* (Washington, D.C.: Congressional Quarterly, 1971), 68.

67. Clark, 116.

ADMINISTRATIVE

POLITICS

"A political system involves all the interrelated institutions and processes by which the decisions of government are made. More specifically, a political system involves actions of persons in many patterned, interrelated roles."[1]

Robert Presthus reminds us that ours is an organizational society.[2] Characterized by a highly advanced division of labor and bureaucratization, modern society places a premium on rationality, effectiveness, and efficiency. By coordinating human activity, organizations are designed to achieve specific goals in ways which emphasize these qualities without producing unsatisfactory consequences. Max Weber's analysis of bureaucracy with its unique qualities of hierarchical authority, division of labor, rules, and career employees, has so influenced our understanding of formal organizations that the terms— "bureaucracy" and "organization"—are often used synonymously.

The administration of criminal justice is no exception to the tendency for increased bureaucratization. As described in Chapter I, there are many and varied subunits, each with its own functions and responsibilities. Recruitment patterns and training are geared toward the development of specialized skills in each of the participants. According to the formal outline of the system, the administration of justice is an orderly continuum in which a variety of professionals act upon the accused in the interest of society.

Alvin Gouldner has discussed the two principal orientations that have been most prevalent in analyses of organizations, the "rational model" and the "natural system model."[3] The rational model, exemplified in the work of Weber, views the organization as an "instrument . . . towards the realization of expressly announced group goals."[4] This model defines authority as an attribute of the office, as distinct from a relationship among the incumbents of formal positions. The emphasis on the legally prescribed structure of the organization implies a "mechanical" system whose parts are rationally coordinated to enhance the efficiency of the whole. Deviations from rationality are assumed to result from random mistakes due to ignorance or error in calculation. Peabody had characterized this concept as the "organization without people approach."[5]

Recently theorists such as Talcott Parsons and Philip Selznick have developed the alternative "natural system model."[6] This model recognizes that the realization of system goals is but one of several important needs which the organization fulfills. The emphasis is upon the adaptive responses that the system makes to meet its needs since informal systems arise to meet the goals of both the organization and its actors.

Social scientists have recognized that discussion of an organization solely in terms of its structure is inadequate for a full appreciation of its dynamic processes. Although the term "organization" suggests a certain bareness, a lean, no-nonsense system of consciously coordinated activities, all organizations are molded by forces tangential to their rationally ordered structures and stated goals. The rules do not completely account for the behavior of the actors since an informal structure also exists which results from the social environment and the interaction of these actors. Organizations have formal decision-making processes, but these may serve mostly to legitimize organizational goals and act to enhance the symbolic needs of authority. Emphasis on the prescribed structure may neglect the fact that the achievement of goals is dependent upon the behavior of actors with their own requirements, which may run counter to the manifest aims of the organization. In addition, it must be recognized that the organization itself has survival needs which have to be fulfilled. Thus the realization of system goals is but one of the several important needs which the organization performs. Important in this conception of administration are the adaptive responses that the system makes to meet its needs since informal systems arise to meet the goals of both the organization and its actors.

Before continuing to develop this conceptual framework of the administration of justice, it is necessary to specify certain assumptions. First, it should be noted that the judicial process is an open system; new cases, changes in organization personnel, and different conditions in the political system mean that it is forced to deal with constant variations in its environment. Second, there is a condition of scarcity within the system. Shortages of resources such as time, information, and personnel are characteristic of bureaucracy. Every case cannot be processed according to the formally prescribed criteria. This affects the subunits of law enforcement—police, prosecutor, courts—so that each competes with the others for the available resources. Central to these ideas is the politics of administration: the range of interactions between an agency and its environment that augment, retain, or diminish the basic resources needed to attain organizational goals.

CRIMINAL CONTROL V. DUE PROCESS

In what is regarded as one of the most important recent contributions to systematic thought about the administration of criminal justice, Herbert Packer has articulated the values supporting two models of the justice process.[7] His schema has the desirable quality of corresponding to the general emphases of the social organization models described above.

Since his "due process model" has features paralleling the "rational model" and his "criminal control model" parallels the "natural system model," their usefulness for analysis is enhanced.

Packer has noted the gulf existing between the "due process model" of criminal administration, with its emphasis on the rights of the individual, and the "criminal control model," which sees the regulation of criminal conduct as the most important function of the judicial system. Where the former adheres to a strict interpretation of the legally prescribed structures characteristic of the rational model of organization, the latter recognizes that the needs of the administrators of the system must be acknowledged. Not only do bureaucrats compete among themselves in the advancement of their goals, but they are also under pressure from elements in the environment as they make decisions. Viewed as a spectrum of normative choice, these polar models allow us to "recognize explicitly the value choices that underlie the details of the criminal process."[8]

Even though Packer describes his models as polar, he recognizes that the administration of justice operates within the environment of contemporary American society; it is therefore influenced by cultural forces which place limits on the lengths to which the models may be taken. There are, then, certain assumptions found in both conceptual frameworks which serve as a common ground for the operation of any criminal justice model. Packer summarizes these cultural forces as follows:

(1) Definition of conduct that may be treated as criminal is separate from and prior to the process of identifying and dealing with persons as criminals.

(2) The criminal process should be invoked only when a crime has been committed and there is a reasonable prospect of apprehending the perpetrator.

(3) The power of government to investigate and apprehend persons suspected of committing crimes is limited.

(4) Certain terms used within the system are based on the idea that the accused is not merely an object to be acted upon but an entity in the process who may force the administrators to

demonstrate to an independent authority (judge and jury) that he is guilty of the charges against him.

These common assumptions are necessary for the partial resolution of the tension between the two models to take place.

The "due process model," often referred to as the "combat or adversary model," is the image generally held by the public of the judicial system. This view stresses both the adversary nature of courtroom proceedings and the rights of the individual as the truth is discovered. Packer compares the "due process model" to an obstacle course, since a determination of guilt may be affirmed only by following certain procedures. Although it does not deny the social desirability of repressing crime, it stresses the problems of errors committed during the fact-finding stages. Because of the value placed upon the individual's freedom, the deprivation of which could result from the judicial process, every effort is made to protect the accused from the consequences of errors in the system. Hence, the model assumes that a person is innocent until proved guilty, that he has an opportunity to discredit the case brought against him, and that an impartial jduge is provided to decide the outcome.

Compared with the "due process model," the "criminal control model" de-emphasizes the adversary nature of the judicial system. Rather than stressing the combative elements of the courtroom, this model notes that bargaining between the state and the accused occurs at several points. The ritual of the courtroom is enacted in only a small number of cases; the rest are disposed of through negotiations over the charges, usually ending with defendants' pleas of guilty. An assumption of this model is that law enforcement officials do not have the resources for the practices extolled by the combat model. To operate efficiently the "criminal control model" acts on the basis of a high rate of apprehension, the sifting out of the innocent, and the conviction of offenders; this demands speed and finality, which depend upon informality and minimizing the occasions for challenge. Hence, the probable guilt is administratively determined primarily on the results of the police investigation and a screening process in which those cases which may not terminate in conviction are filtered out of the system. At each successive stage, from arrest to arraignment, preliminary hearing, and courtroom trial, a series of routinized procedures is used by a variety of judicial actors to determine if the accused should be passed on to the next level.

The general public probably understands the legal system in ways embodied by the rational or due process model. Its view is consistent with Arnold's conception of the "Ideal of Law Enforcement," in which principles, instead of personal discretion, control the actions of judges and prosecutors.[9] The public's estimate of the judicial system is that of an on-going mechanistic process in which infractions of statutes are discovered, defendants indicted, and punishments imposed, with little reference to either the needs of the system or of the individualization of justice. Hence, the belief exists that the rules of the organization are strictly applied, with little discretion in the administration of the machine. As Arnold indicates, any attempt to induce flexibility into the system must be carried out sub rosa, since a purpose of the process is to dramatize the moral values of the community.

The existence of these two models has numerous policy implications. One might suggest that during periods of low criminal activity the system can tolerate attention to due process values, while at times when the public is aroused by rising crime rates, greater emphasis would be placed on the criteria of the criminal control model. Similarly it would appear that defendants with money, position, and influence are able to insist that the due process rules be maintained, while the poor are handled without regard to their rights. The models have definite implications for those policymakers interested in reforming the administration of criminal justice. Without an assessment of the reality of the system, efforts toward social change are doomed. Increasing the due process safeguards concerning the admittance of certain types of evidence in the courtroom will have little influence if only a small number of defendants avail themselves of the right to trial.

DECISION-MAKING IN AN EXCHANGE SYSTEM

While observing the interrelated activities of the organizations in the legal process one might ask: "Why do these agencies cooperate?" "If the police refuse to transfer information to the prosecutor concerning the commission of a crime, what are the rewards or sanctions which might be given or imposed?" "Is it possible that organizations maintain a form of 'bureaucratic accounting' which, in a sense, keeps track of the resources allocated to an agency and the support which is returned?" "How are cues transmitted from one agency to another to influence decision-making?" These are some of the questions posed when decisions are viewed as an output of an exchange system.

William Gore notes that it is possible to look at a system as a network of interdependent interests. In place of the traditional assumptions that the agency is supported by statutory authority, his view recognizes that an organization has many clients with which it interacts and upon whom it is dependent for certain resources. It is understood that formal organizations are imbedded "in an environment of other organizations as well as in a complex of norms, values and collectivities of the society."[10] An important aspect of this view is the recognition that an organization is to some degree dependent upon its environment; it is a subsystem of a more inclusive system.

As interdependent subunits of a system, an organization and its clients are engaged in a set of exchanges across their boundaries. Exchange is modeled on the economic concept of the market in which inputs and outputs, or resources and products, are exchanged among persons and systems. The judicial system may be viewed as a set of inter-organizational exchange relationships. In this system a number of agencies contribute to the achievement of system goals—the disposition of criminal law violations. In turn, the interdependence of organizations influences the setting of goals. "A continuing situation of necessary interaction between an organization and its environment introduces an element of environmental control into the organization."[11]

From this viewpoint the judicial system is analogous to what Long has called a community game.[12] The participants in the judicial system (game) share a territorial field and collaborate for different and particular ends. The complex of organizations in the justice game may be seen as a system, with its parts varying in the kind and frequency of their relations with each other and the larger system—the community.

Within the judicial system some of the subunits are obvious; their relationships and goals need be only briefly mentioned. Many of the exchange relationships in the administration of justice are necessitated not only by the needs of the system, but by the statutory requirements which demand participation by various parts of the system in decision-making. The police, charged with making decisions concerning the apprehension of suspects, interact with the prosecutor's office when presenting evidence and recommending charges. The defendant, through his counsel, may exchange a guilty plea for a reduction by the prosecutor of the charges. Likewise, the courts and prosecutor are linked by the decision to bring charges, the activities in the courtroom, and disposition of the case. Besides these key organizations, there are other judicial agencies, rehabilitation units, and informal groups which are part of the process but which participate only periodically. Although mere interaction does not of necessity mean that exchange will occur, these social contacts lead to the development of relations in which the aim of each participant is to safeguard his own interests. Through the recognition of these interests exchanges may be developed which will benefit both partners.

Not all units of the judicial system are activated in every case; some parts are more closely tied to the achievement of system goals than are others. Gouldner has emphasized the need to differentiate system parts on the basis of their relative dependence upon other parts. Certain subunits are very dependent since they do not have well-developed access to resources outside the system, whereas others have a high degree of functional autonomy. The prosecuting attorney, for instance, is a key figure in the administration of justice since, under our concept of public prosecution, other units may not act unless he has decided to bring charges against the suspect. It should also be stressed that the units of a system are not engaged in relations which are necessarily symmetrical.

Participation of an organization in the judicial system is related to the perceived domain of the agencies. Although clear delineation of domain as defined by statute may be a primary aim of the "rational model," in the real world competition may exist among agencies over jurisdiction. For instance, domain between the county prosecutor's office and the United States Attorney's office in the disposition of auto theft or narcotics cases is often unclear. The achievement of domain consensus requires negotiations when functions of interacting organizations are not clearly delineated. This may be a prerequisite to exchange. As Levine and White indicate:

> These processes of achieving domain consensus constitute much of the interaction between organizations. While they may not involve the immediate flow of elements, they are often necessary preconditions for the exchange of elements, because without at least minimal domain consensus there can be no exchange among organizations."[13]

By viewing the administration of justice as a system of inter-organizational relations, it is possible to select one agency and view the network from that perspective. Alternatively, one may note the influence of decisions made in one agency on the relationships and decisions made in the other parts of the judicial process. Merton's concept of the "role set" has been adapted as a device for the study of inter-organizational relations.[14] A role set is made up of the roles and role relationships associated with a particular status. In each behavioral relationship the judicial actor plays different roles, even though he continues to interact with reference to his official status. Thus, the police activate different role behaviors when they interact with the prosecutor, judge, defense lawyer, and community leader.

As shown in Figure II-1, we can look at the office of prosecuting attorney as a focal organization and consider its "organizational set" with reference to the other agencies, groups, and persons with which it interacts. From the earlier

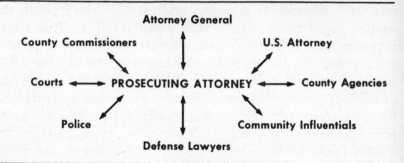

Figure II-1: SELECTED EXCHANGE RELATIONSHIPS OF THE PROSECUTOR

discussion, it is apparent that the organization set is made up of the clients of the office, those subunits of the judicial system which interact with the office of prosecuting attorney in decision-making. Conflicting demands by members of the organization set may be handled in ways similar to devices used to ameliorate role conflict. These may include organizational segregation and the development of formal rules.

The concepts of an exchange system may also be used to understand the influence of decisions made in one agency on the relationships and decisions made in the other parts of the judicial process. As shown in Figure II-2, these lateral relationships are necessary because the outputs of one subsystem of the administration of justice become the inputs of the next unit. A judge's decision to convict a felon affects the arresting officer's effectiveness record, the prosecutor's conviction rate, and the credence of the sentencing recommendation of the probation officer. An official's decisions are often anticipatory of the judge's reactions. Lenient sentences or fines for certain types of offenses may discourage the police from making these arrests.

One of the more interesting examples of this interdependence was given to the author by a district court judge who noted that

Police ⟷ Prosecutor ⟷ Defense ⟷ Court ⟷ Corrections

Figure II-2: SELECTED LATERAL RELATIONSHIPS IN THE ADMINISTRATION OF JUSTICE

when the number of prisoners reached the "riot" point, the warden urged the courts to slow down the flow. This meant that men were let out on parole and that the number of persons given probation and suspended sentences increased. One could speculate that the prosecutor viewing this behavior on the part of the judges would reduce the inputs to the court system either by not preferring charges or by increasing the pressure for guilty pleas through bargaining. Adjustments of other parts of the system could be expected to follow. For instance, the police might sense the lack of interest of the prosecutor in accepting charges, and hence they may be willing to send only "airtight" cases to him for indictment.

Recent events in which judicial systems have been placed under extreme pressures, such as the Detroit riots of 1967, the New York City prison riots of 1970, and the Mayday demonstrations in Washington during 1971 should provide fertile arenas for social science investigations. In each situation elements of the administration of justice responded to overload in the system by setting aside formal due process criteria and improvising, through informal adjustments, measures to relieve these pressures. Observers of the arraignment of the thousands of defendants arrested during the Detroit riots noted that the judicial system responded with: "high bail, absence of counsel, failure to consider individual circumstances, failure to inform defendants of their constitutional rights, and an emphasis on expediency."[15] Similarly, when prisoners in New York complained of overcrowded conditions, special bail hearings were set up to relieve the pressures. The charges against most of those arrested in Washington, D.C., during Mayday, 1971, were dropped.

The Nature of Exchange

Before proceeding it is necessary to clarify the concept of exchange. Social scientists have used this term in a number of contexts to describe a variety of phenomena. Hence one might raise questions about the nature of exchange, its proximity to bargaining, and the conditions under which exchange occurs.

The type of resources transferred and the structural context of this activity need to be understood.

Formally stated, *exchange is an activity involving the transfer of resources between organizations and individuals which has consequences for the common achievement of goals.* A partial list of the elements transferred between parts of the legal process: support for the actions of decision makers, policy commitments, material resources (labor, supplies, equipment), and information. As Blau notes, two conditions are required for exchange: (1) an orientation toward ends that can be attained only through interaction with other persons; and (2) the need to adapt means to further the achievement of these ends. A person who supplies rewarding services to another obligates him. To discharge this obligation the latter must in turn furnish benefits to the former. The continuation of exchange relationships generates trust between the actors and promotes a cooperative attitude which is enhanced by the reward structure of the organization. "Hence, processes of social exchange, which may originate in pure self-interest, generate trust in social relations through their recurrent and gradually expanding character."[16]

Opportunities for exchange are enhanced when conflict is over interests rather than values. Where there is a conflict of interest, the type of exchange is such

> "that solutions may be reached by an interaction which seems competitive, but since the parties are not morally involved in the result the interests are in fact not diametrically opposed."[17]

Exchange may take the form of either (A) cooperation or (B) bargaining. The difference between these forms hinges upon the question, "Were the conditions for the transfer of resources negotiated?"

A. Cooperation. —The parties each recognize that it is in their interest to agree to the movement of resources across organizational boundaries, without the need for negotiations concerning the transfer. This is similar to what might be called non-negotiated decision-making. It is based on common expectations, with the implicit understanding that cooperation is mutually advantageous to the interests of the parties. Cooperation will probably occur when there is little room for misunderstanding between the parties concerning the transfer of resources.[18] A cooperative exchange between the prosecutor and a court official may be an agreement to delay a trial while new evidence is gathered. The ready acceptance of the court official to this change, without setting conditions, would distinguish this type of exchange. This does not rule out the possibility that cooperation on the surface may, in fact, be a ploy by the agreeing partner to use this exchange as a basis for bargaining in the future.

  B. Bargaining.—Negotiations between the participants are conducted over the conditions under which resources will be transferred. As Dahl and Lindblom have written, "Leaders bargain because they disagree and expect that future agreement is possible and will be profitable."[19] Bargaining occurs when the contenders expect to achieve mutually profitable adjustments and recognize that neither can emerge supreme—a nonzero-sum game.

  Bargaining, therefore, involves a strategy of compromise: a system of incentives by which all parties are brought to agree to the (final) settlement. In bargaining an actor may be concerned with the "gratification-deprivation balance of his end system as a whole," over a period of time and on many issues.[20] Thus, the terms of the bargain may be unrelated to the immediate issue.

  Bargaining may result in agreement with terms which are either implicit or explicit. Under conditions of implicit bargaining the terms of the exchange may not be formally acknowledged; however, there are expectations by both parties about the pay-offs for exchange. Implicit bargains are characteristic of exchange between formal organizations when interactions are relatively frequent and when norms oppose the arrangement. In the administration of justice, the parties to a negotiated plea of guilty maintain the myth that the defendant has not been promised special considerations.[21] In plea bargaining situations negotiations are usually concluded with a statement by the prosecutor to the effect that "I'll see what I can do." The attorney for the accused usually responds, "Fine, and I'm sure that everything can be worked out all right." The actors have completed their bargain, but are trying to maintain the fiction that the formal criterion of the law is being met. This type of bargaining necessitates some guarantee that the favor will be returned, or that the actors will be required to bargain again in the future.

In speaking about interactions between organizations, we must remember that they are "the resultants of the decisions and actions of concrete persons acting in roles."[22] Exchanges do not simply "sail" from one subsystem to another, but take place in an institutionalized setting which may be compared to a market. In the market, decisions are made between persons occupying boundary-spanning roles who set the conditions under which the exchange will occur.[23] In the judicial system this may mean that a representative of the parole board agrees to forward a recommendation to the judge, or it could mean that there is extended plea bargaining between a deputy prosecutor and a defense attorney.

Exchange relations are enhanced by the fact that the administration of justice is characterized by the extensive decentralization of discretionary power. Each patrolman is able to make his own decisions regarding arrest in most circumstances involving minor crimes. The decision to prosecute is frequently in the hands of the individual deputy prosecutor as a result of his exchanges with individual policemen and criminal lawyers. In one prosecutor's office this practice was terminated when it became obvious that exchange hinged upon the proclivities of each deputy. The practice of police and criminal lawyers' "shopping around" for an agreeable deputy seriously interfered with the goals of the office.

THE POLITICS OF ADMINISTRATION

According to Norton Long, the saddest sight in the administrative world is an agency "possessed of statutory life, armed with paralysis and deprived of power."[24] In an exchange system, power is largely dependent upon the ability of an

organization to create clientele relationships which will support
and enhance its needs, for although interdependence is characteristic of the judicial system, competition with other public
agencies for support also exists. Since organizations operate in
an economy of scarcity, faced with more claims than they can
fulfill with available resources, the organization must exist in a
favorable power position in relation to its clientele.

Reciprocal and unique claims are made by the organization
and its clients. Thus, rather than being oriented toward one
public, an organization is beholden to several publics, some
visible and others seen only from the pinnacle of leadership. As
Gore notes, when these claims are "firmly anchored inside the
organization and the lines drawn taut, the tensions between
conflicting claims form a net serving as the institutional base for
the organization."[25] In its relationship with other system
units, each part of the administration of justice must be able to
solve its functional problems by strengthening client relationships, by repelling cooptive threats, and by securing support.
Since each organization's goals are affected by the environment,
each must keep its "organizational ear" to the ground, ready to
detect threats to its power and other changes which may
portend downward budgetary modifications. It must appear to
be performing a valuable service to the public, and must be able
to demonstrate the organization's abilities through records of
achievement.

Schelling has noted that publicity surrounding an exchange
may influence the type of interorganizational relationship.

> "If one party has a 'public' and the other has not, the latter may try
> to neutralize his disadvantage by excluding the relevant public; or if
> both parties fear the potentialities for stalemate in the simultaneous
> use of this tactic, they may try to enforce an agreement on
> secrecy."[26]

Because members of the judicial system believe that the general
public subscribes to the combat or due process model of law
enforcement, negotiations concerning the decision to prosecute,
law enforcement policies, and sentencing decisions are conducted in secret. In such exchange relationships there is often
the potential for one member to use the threat of exposure as a

ploy in bargaining. This may cause judicial actors to "cover" their acts so that they cannot be held responsible for decisions which they feel might provoke criticism. Prosecutors may seek a high bail in cases which have attracted public attention because they want the judge to take responsibility for setting the defendant free. At the same time there exists a norm within the system toward secrecy. This is enforced through the complicated web by which decision makers are bound to the system. The true nature of routine operations thought to be sensitive is shielded from public view.

The power of an organization may be enhanced by the variety of clientele claims made upon it. These in turn provide greater opportunities for strengthening the organization in resource exchanges. A diversity of clientele-publics may give the organization greater freedom to maneuver within the system, handling threats by playing one client against the other.

Although the formal structures of the judicial process stress antagonistic and competitive subunits, the interaction of exchange may strengthen cooperation within the system, thus deflecting it from its manifest goals. For example, although the prosecutor and defense counsel occupy roles which are prescribed as antagonistic, continued interaction on the job, in professional associations, and political or social groups, may produce a friendship which greatly influences role playing. Combat in the courtroom, as ordained by the formal structure, may not only endanger the personal relationship, but it may also expose weaknesses in the actors to their own clienteles. Rather than the unpredictability and professional insecurity stressed by the system, decisions on cases may be made to benefit mutually the actors in the exchange.

Thus far, four major aspects of the conceptual framework have been presented. It has been postulated that the justice system is composed of a number of subunits and clientele groups which exist in a political and social environment. Exchanges between the subunits and their clienteles are necessary for the adaptation of the system and the achievement of its goals. By viewing the judicial system from the perspective of the focal organization, the set of agencies and individuals which interact with each subunit are considered part of the decisional process. Finally, it has been suggested that decision-making is a product of the system and its exchanges.

CRIMINAL JUSTICE AS A FILTERING SYSTEM

The President's Commission on Law Enforcement and Administration of Justice has referred to the legal process as a continuum—an orderly progression of events.[27] Like all legally constituted structures there are formally designated points in the process where decisions are made concerning the disposition of cases. As described in the previous chapter, a series of law enforcement and judicial actors are involved in the decisions made as the defendant's case is considered. To speak of the system as a continuum, however, may underplay the complexity and the flux of relationships within it; although the administration of criminal justice is composed of a set of subsystems, there are no formal provisions for the subordination of one unit to another. Each has its own clientele, goals, and norms, yet the outputs of one unit constitute the inputs to another.

What the commission correctly notes is that the criminal justice process resembles a filter through which cases are screened: some are advanced to the next level of decision-making, while others are either rejected or the conditions under which they are processed are changed. On the basis of the limited statistics available it appears that "approximately one half of those arrested are dismissed by the police, prosecutor, or magistrate at an early stage of the case."[28] Other evidence is equally impressive. Sobel found (Table II-1) that 62 percent of the adult felony arrests in Kings County, New York, resulted in either a dismissal or reduction to a misdemeanor before the case went to the grand jury for indictment. In Detroit's Recorder's Court, prosecution was instituted in only 60 percent of the 46,800 cases.[29]

The Rand Institute recently announced the results of an examination of the New York City Criminal Court, one of the most extensive studies of the administration of justice in a

TABLE II-1
CASE MORTALITY: ADULT FELONY ARRESTS
KING COUNTY, NEW YORK, 1960-1962 (in percentages)

Stage of Process	Number	Totals	Remaining
Preliminary arraignment—lower criminal court	32,000	100	100
Discharged, dismissed, or adjusted at preliminary arraignment	2,000	6.2	93.8
Dismissed on merits at preliminary arraignment	6,000	18.6	75.2
Reduced to misdemeanor at preliminary arraignment	12,000	37.6	37.6
Held for grand jury	12,000	37.6	37.6
Dismissed by grand jury	1,000	3.1	34.5
Reduced by grand jury	1,000	3.1	31.4
Indictments found	10,000	31.4	31.4
Indictments dismissed by trial courts not on merits	320	1.0	30.4
Indictments dismissed by trial courts on merits	640	2.0	28.4
Adjudged youthful offender	860	2.6	25.8
Pleas to felony	3,200	10.0	15.8
Pleas to misdemeanor	4,280	13.4	2.4
Verdict of felony	350	1.2	1.3
Verdict of misdemeanor	50	.3	1.0
Verdict of not guilty	300	1.0	0.0

SOURCE: Nathan R. Sobel, "Crime in New York City," Brooklyn Law Review, 30 (December, 1963): 13.

single city. It found that the court processed approximately 330,000 cases, yet 90,000 never went beyond the preliminary examination because the cases were dismissed or transferred to other jurisdictions, or the defendants not located. Indeed, 15,565 cases were "lost." Only 7 percent of the 200,000 found guilty received a trial; sentences were imposed on the rest following a plea of guilty. Commenting on the report Subin noted, "the system has been almost totally directed toward disposing of cases without trial. We cling to the due-process idea of justice, and it doesn't exist any more."[30]

Organizations exist within a social context in which the subunits and men find some activities rewarding and others strain-producing. As social theorists have told us, the policies of a bureaucratic system will evolve so that they will maximize the rewards, while minimizing the strains for the organization. The administration of justice is greatly affected by the values of each decision maker, whose career, influence, and position may be more important than are considerations for the formal requirements of the law. This means that accommodations will be sought with those in the exchange system so that decisions can be made which are consistent with the values of the participants and the organization. Hence, a wide variety of departures from the strictures of the due process model are accepted by the actors in the justice system but are never publicly acknowledged. Because of the strain caused by the large number of cases processed by the system, and the adversary nature of the due process model, members of the bureaucracy can reduce stress while maximizing rewards by filtering out those cases which are viewed as disruptive or a potential threat to the established norms.

Because they fear they will be criticized for committing these "work crimes," the members of the criminal justice system are bound together into an effective network of complicity. As Blumberg says, "This consists of a work arrangement in which the patterned, covert, informal breaches and evasions of due process are institutionalized, but are, nevertheless, denied to exist."[31] This may explain why judicial actors are almost pathologically distrustful of those outsiders who are able to view decision-making. What is often seen is an administrative system which is trying to deal with a large number of tension-producing strains. As Skolnick notes, a whole language with nuances known only to system actors has emerged within the administration of justice to deal with these strains.

> "Thus 'cooperation' implies an understanding of the requirements of the other functionaries in the system, 'ability' implies the capacity to fulfill those needs, and 'rationality' or 'reasonableness' suggests the acceptance of prevailing assumptions."[32]

A central role in the administration of criminal justice is played by the prosecuting attorney. His are the strategic moves: he recommends bail, selects the charges, chooses the judges, and determines if a lesser plea will be accepted. Although discretion is a formal power of the prosecutor, it is exercised within the exchange framework of a bureaucratic system. In addition, the highly partisan nature of his office in most jurisdictions can mean that political considerations are prominent in decision-making. Therefore, exchange relationships, "the norms of efficiency, good public relations, and the maintenance of harmony and *esprit de corps* among his underlings" will greatly influence this power.[33]

At each stage of prosecutorial decision-making there are a number of alternatives which may be applied. Like many administrative processes, however, the closer a case moves to trial, the less latitude is available to decision makers. Blumberg discerns a sieve-like operation in which a case is handled in an increasingly finite manner as it is transferred from the initial point of police handling to a preliminary hearing and trial.[34] At each succeeding step in the process more judicial personnel are associated with the case and there is a greater intricacy in the formal requirements of the system. As a case moves toward the courtroom, the visibility of decision-making increases and the exchange relationships of participants become more involved. Because of the complexity of the organizations of criminal justice and the high degree of interdependence among actors with discretionary jobs, decisions have a compounding effect on other participants in the system. Under these circumstances the freedom of the prosecutor, the accused, and the court to find a mutually beneficial solution is constricted.

In a study of the Office of King County Prosecutor (Seattle), the author found that during the initial phases of the administration of justice, persons handling cases tended to recommend higher charges than were eventually filed.[35] Often the police confronted the deputy prosecutor with a recommendation that the accused be charged with multiple offenses. As the case was reviewed in the prosecutor's office, there was a tendency to reduce the charges to those which could be expected to result in conviction. And as the actors in the decision-making process assumed a greater responsibility for prosecuting the case in the uncharted ground of the courtroom, they became more conservative in their charging recommendations. Deputies did not want to suggest charges for cases they might have to prosecute in court with results which might reflect unfavorably on their abilities, yet they were also under pressures from the police to take cases, thus relieving the law enforcement load.

Of central concern is the treatment of defendants in this administrative process. Since defendants pass through the system while the judicial actors remain, the accused may become secondary figures in the bureaucratic setting. The defendant and his case may be viewed as a challenge or temporarily disruptive influences by the actors in the administration of justice. The tensions which individual cases may produce are repressed because system personnel must be able to interact on the basis of exchange in the future. Since these relations must be maintained, pressures may be brought to dispose of cases in a manner which will help to sustain the existing linkages within the system.

Although the empirical evidence does not yet exist, social scientists have expressed the fear that defendants with certain social characteristics who are accused of certain types of crimes receive unfair treatment because of the bureaucratic rather than the adversary emphasis within the justice process. One suspects that those persons who can be handled without creating strain will receive harsher treatment than those who because of their status might be viewed as a threat to maintenance of productive exchange relationships. As William Chambliss suggests:

> "Those persons are arrested, tried, and sentenced who can offer the fewest rewards for nonenforcement of the laws and who can be processed without creating any undue strain for the organizations which comprise the legal system."[36]

The screening process also depends upon the negotiating skill of the accused's counsel. By exposing weaknesses in the state's case, he may convince the prosecutor of the futility of proceeding to trial. Alternatively, counsel may help to convince the defendant of the strength of the case against him and urge that he bargain for a lesser charge in exchange for a guilty plea.

In some jurisdictions the screening process works so well that, statistically, if the prosecutor says a person is guilty, he is. From the standpoint of the model presented here, the courts, to an increasing extent, become "tribunals of last resort" after the administrators of the system have made their decisions.

Interviews with prosecutors, court officials, and defense attorneys indicate that the values of the administrative or criminal control model are widely held by participants in the judicial process.[37] The tenor of comments by these actors reveals that the conditions under which decisions are made contribute to the assumption and reinforcement of these values. A number of respondents mentioned that they were constantly dealing with the same type of "lower class scum." As one experienced deputy prosecutor said:

> "We know that more than eighty per cent of these guys are guilty. After a while you get so that you can look at the sheet [the case record] and tell what is going to happen."

Similar attitudes were expressed by judges of the lower trial courts and those attorneys dependent upon criminal cases for a major portion of their work. It is startling to hear a judge say that he assumed that defendants surviving the scrutiny of the police and prosecutor must be guilty.

As emphasized throughout this chapter, the administration of criminal justice may be viewed as an organization with goals antagonistic to the due process or adversary model. Decisions concerning the disposition of cases are influenced by the selective nature of a filtering process in which administrative discretion and interpersonal exchange relationships are extremely important. At each level of decision-making actors are able to determine which types of crimes shall come to official notice, which kinds of offenders will be processed, and the degree of enthusiasm which will be brought to seeking a conviction.

> "It is in the day-to-day practices and policies of the processing agencies that the law is put into effect and it is out of the struggle to perform their tasks in ways which maximize rewards and minimize strains for the organization and the individuals involved that the legal processing agencies shape the law."[38]

This framework suggests a number of questions which should be investigated as the next step in the research process; points which will concern us in the remainder of this book: How does case-load input affect decision-making at each level? What are the congruent role relationships played by actors in the exchange process? How do a defendant's characteristics influence decision-making? What types of cases arrive in the courts? It is only when questions such as these are answered that we can begin to plan for the more effective utilization of the criminal justice process and erect safeguards to protect the constitutional rights of citizens.

NOTES

1. Charles R. Adrian and Charles Press, *The American Political Process* (New York: McGraw-Hill, 1965), 11.

2. Robert Presthus, *The Organizational Society* (New York: Knopf, 1962).

3. Alvin W. Gouldner, "Organizational Analysis," *Sociology Today: Problems and Prospects,* ed. Robert K. Merton, Leonard Broom, and Leonard S. Cottrell (New York: Basic Books, 1959), 400-428.

4. Ibid., 404.

5. Robert Peabody, *Organizational Authority* (New York: Atherton, 1964), 18.

6. Talcott Parsons, "Suggestions for a Sociological Theory of Organizations," Administrative Science Quarterly, 1 (1956), 63-85, 225-239; Philip Selznick, *Leadership in Administration* (Evanston: Row Peterson, 1957).

7. Originally published as "Two Models of the Criminal Process," University of Pennsylvania Law Review, 113 (1964), 1-68, it also appears in Packer's book, *The Limits of the Criminal Sanction* (Stanford: Stanford University Press, 1968). References are from the book. Criticism of this work is found in John Griffiths, "Ideology in Criminal Procedure or a Third 'Model' of the Criminal Process," Yale Law Journal, 79 (1970), 359.

8. Ibid., 153.

9. Thurman Arnold, *The Symbols of Government* (New Haven: Yale University Press, 1935), 162.

10. William J. Gore, *Administrative Decision-Making: A Heuristic Model* (New York: John Wiley and Sons, 1964), 22.

11. William M. Evan, "Toward a Theory of Inter-Organizational Relations," Management Science, 11 (1965), B-218.

12. Norton Long, "The Local Community as an Ecology of Games," *The Polity,* ed. Norton Long (Chicago: Rand McNally, 1962), 142.

13. Sol Levine and Paul E. White, "Exchange as a Conceptual Framework for the Study of Interorganizational Relationships," Administrative Science Quarterly, 5 (1961), 583-601 See also: Peter Blau, *Exchange and Power in Social Life* (New York:

John Wiley, 1964); George C. Homans, *Social Behavior: Its Elementary Forms* (New York: Harcourt, Brace and World, 1961).

14. Evan, B-220; Robert Merton, *Social Theory and Social Structure* (New York: Free Press, 1967), 368.

15. "The Administration of Justice in the Wake of the Detroit Civil Disorder of July, 1967," Michigan Law Review, 66 (1968), 1542-1629. See also: "Criminal Justice in Extremis: Administration of Justice during the April 1968 Chicago Disorder," University of Chicago Law Review, 36 (1969), 455.

16. Blau, *Exchange and Power*, 4.

17. Brian Grosman, *The Prosecutor* (Toronto: University of Toronto Press, 1969), 87.

18. Stewart Macaulay, "Non-Contractual Relations in Business: A Preliminary Study," American Sociological Review, 28 (1963), 55.

19. Robert A. Dahl and Charles E. Lindblom, *Politics, Economics and Welfare* (New York: Harper and Brothers, 1953), 326. For the most fully developed discussion of bargaining see Thomas C. Schelling, *The Strategy of Conflict* (Cambridge: Harvard University Press, 1960), ch. II.

20. Martin Meyerson and Edward Banfield, *Politics, Planning and the Public Interest* (New York: Free Press, 1955), 309.

21. Lewis A. Froman, Jr., *People and Politics* (Englewood Cliffs: Prentice-Hall, 1962), 55.

22. William Mitchell, *Sociological Analysis and Politics: The Theories of Talcott Parsons* (Englewood Cliffs: Prentice Hall, 1967), 79.

23. James D. Thompson, "Organizations and Output Transactions," American Journal of Sociology, 68 (1962), 309.

24. Long, "Power and Administration," The Polity, 50-63.

25. Gore, 22.

26. Schelling, 29.

27. U.S. President's Commission on Law Enforcement and Administration of Justice, *The Challenge of Crime in a Free Society* (1967), 7.

28. President's Commission, 133.

29. President's Commission, *Task Force Report: The Courts*, 130.

30. Lesley Oelsner, "Criminal Courts: Statistical Profile," New York Times, March 28, 1970. See also: Dallin Oaks and Warren Lehman, *A Criminal Justice System and the Indigent* (Chicago: University of Chicago Press, 1967), 46.

31. Abraham Blumberg, "The Practice of Law as a Confidence Game, Organizational Cooptation of a Profession," Law and Society Review, 1 (June, 1967), 15-39.

32. Jerome Skolnick, "Social Control in the Adversary System," Journal of Conflict Resolution, 11 (March, 1967), 63.

33. David Matza, *Delinquency and Drift* (New York: John Wiley, 1964), 122.

34. Blumberg, *Criminal Justice* (Chicago: Quadrangle, 1967), 50.

35. George F. Cole, "The Politics of Prosecution: The Decision to Prosecute" (Unpublished Ph.D. dissertation, University of Washington, 1968).

36. William Chambliss, *Crime and the Legal Process* (New York: McGraw-Hill, 1969), 84.

37. Cole, 237.

38. Chambliss, 86.

POLICE

"A democracy, like all other societies, needs order and security, but it also and equally requires civil liberty. This complexity of needs creates difficult theoretical and practical problems."[1]

Although it is currently popular for some politicians to stress the need for "law and order," the complexity of this phrase has not been well explicated. Too often those using it do so without recognizing that two important, yet rather distinct concepts are involved. Law and order is not a new conceptual problem but has been a focus for discussion since the formation of police forces. Society, having given power to the police to arrest and incarcerate citizens, must control this power so that civil liberties are not infringed. If one looks to Magna Carta, one recognizes the limitations placed upon the constables and bailiffs of thirteenth-century England. Without reading between the lines of this ancient document, one can surmise that police abuses, the maintenance of order, and the rule of law were dilemmas similar to those of today.[2]

Packer's concepts of the criminal control model and the due process model are most appropriate as we address ourselves to the role of the police in a democratic society.[3] Yet we must also recognize that the police are but one organization within the closely interrelated system of criminal justice. Their activities are greatly influenced both by the wider political environment and the bureaucratic nature of legal administration, thus adding a third dimension to the dilemma of law and order. Not only is order to be maintained under law, but law enforcement is performed within the context of an organizational system where discretion, culture, and bureaucratic politics affect police operations. Jerome Skolnick well summarizes these problems:

> "The police in democratic society are required to maintain order and to do so under the rule of law. As functionaries charged with maintaining order, they are part of the bureaucracy. The ideology of democratic bureaucracy emphasizes initiative rather than disciplined adherence to rules and regulations. By contrast, the rule of law emphasizes the rights of individual citizens and constraints upon the initiative of legal officials. This tension between the operational consequences of ideas of order, efficiency, and initiative, on the one hand, and legality, on the other, constitutes the principal problem of police as a democratic legal organization."[4]

If the police were to be given the necessary resources, it would be possible to maintain a high level of order in society. Not only would such a policy of "total enforcement" make life intolerable, but it would almost surely preclude the maintenance of civil liberties. In reality, although laws are written as if "total enforcement" were expected, the police determine the outer limits of "actual enforcement" throughout the criminal process.[5] Decisions are made to enforce certain laws but not others, because of a number of factors: the difficulty of making arrests, the resources needed to obtain evidence, disagreement in the community as to whether certain acts should be considered unlawful, and the pressure from persons with influence who desire that some laws not be enforced. These "low visibility" choices by police administrators are one of the political ingredients in the criminal justice system. Law enforcement agencies are faced with fulfilling their obligations under the law, yet with doing so in ways which will maintain community and organizational support. As part of a bureaucratic structure they resolve the dilemma by establishing procedures which minimize strains and which provide the greatest promise of rewards for the organization and the persons involved.

The functions of the police are more complex than most of us assume. Not only are they charged with maintaining order, enforcing the law, and providing a variety of social services, but the policies which they follow dictate the persons and offenses which will be labeled deviant. If we predicate, as did Durkheim, that no society is free of crime, the determination of policies which allocate resources and set criteria for law enforcement goals becomes an important variable.[6] This consideration was well stated by the President's Commission when it noted:

> "The police must make important judgments about what conduct is in fact criminal; about the allocation of scarce resources; and about the gravity of each individual incident and the proper steps that should be taken."[7]

In a heterogeneous society such as the United States there are bound to be differing interpretations of deviance. Should emphasis be placed upon "upperworld crimes" like the price-fixing conspiracy between General Electric and Westinghouse, or upon "organized crime" so often discussed by J. Edgar Hoover, or upon "low-level" violations such as public drunkenness, shoplifting, and crimes without victims.[8] Each of these categories involves different social classes, different perceptions of deviance, and different modes of enforcement. Each type of deviation will embody different threats and rewards for criminal justice organizations.

Much of the discussion of crime rates shows the influence of law enforcement policy and the role of the police in the justice system. As pointed out earlier, the amount of crime known to the police is a small portion of that which is committed. Presumably they are aware that the law enforcement position is enhanced by the way certain types of offenders are processed. In terms of volume and the generation of public support, the arrest of narcotics offenders or prostitutes have more "pay-off" than the pursuit of "white-collar" criminals. Also, changes in

enforcement methods, such as the introduction of computer-
ized reporting systems, can have a great impact on crime rates.
The rising crime rate during the past decade has been affected
by the fact that cases previously "handled" by the patrolman
on the beat are now reported through formal channels, with the
disposition recorded.

Even before an arrest is made the police have formulated
rules which will influence the level and type of enforcement.
Since the police are the entry point to the criminal justice
system, the total picture is greatly shaped by the decisions made
by officials as to the allocation of resources and their
perception of the level of law enforcement desired by the
community.

POLICE FUNCTIONS

The distinction between order maintenance and law enforcement is important for an understanding of the role of the police
in the administration of justice.[9] Although we usually think
of the police in relation to arrests which follow the breaking of
the laws protecting persons and property, it may be argued that
their principal function is to maintain peace in the community.
Especially when we study the role of the patrolman, the most
numerous officer, we can see he is primarily concerned with
behavior that either disturbs or threatens to disturb the peace.
In these situations the patrolman confronts the public in
ambiguous circumstances and is given wide discretion in matters
of life and death. Law enforcement concerns a violation of the
law when only guilt must be assessed. Order maintenance,
however, usually involves a legal infraction, but there may be a
dispute on the interpretation of right conduct and the assignment of blame.

Bittner's study of the police on skid row is a good example of
the order maintenance function.[10] Walking the streets, the
patrolman may be variously required to help persons in trouble,
control crowds, supervise certain licensed services, and assist
those who are not fully accountable for what they do. In all of
his actions the policeman is not subject to external control and

has the power, if necessary, to arrest, yet also the freedom not to do so.

Some may argue that it is impossible to separate the policeman's "law officer" and "peace officer" roles. However, as Wilson notes, "To the patrolman, 'enforcing the law' is what he does when there is no dispute—when making an arrest or issuing a summons exhausts his responsibilities."[11] Studies made of citizen complaints and service requests justify this emphasis on the order maintenance function of the police. In addition, this orientation and the patrolman's responsibilities cast a long shadow over the internal operations of most police forces.

While we may stress the order maintenance role of the police, we should not forget two other functions which the modern department performs—law enforcement and service. As touched upon before, the law enforcement function is concerned with those situations where the law has been violated and where only guilt needs to be assessed: crimes without victims and such law violations as burglary or murder. Policemen charged with responsibilities in these areas are in the specialized branches of modern departments such as the vice squad and the burglary detail.

In our complex society the police are increasingly called upon to perform a number of services for the population. One study of a metropolitan force showed that more than half the calls coming routinely to the complaint desk were for help or support in connection with personal and interpersonal problems.[12] In Detroit, Bercal found that only 16 percent of the calls to the police for assistance were crime-related.[13] Since the police are usually the only representative of local government which is readily accessible 24 hours every day, they are the agency to which people turn in times of trouble. Many departments provide information, operate ambulance services, locate missing persons, check locks on the homes of vacationers, and stop would-be suicides. In cities the poor and the ignorant, those groups that few are anxious to serve, rely primarily on the police to perform these functions.

Wilson believes that because of the orientation of police

administrators the internal organization of metropolitan departments stress the law enforcement function.[14] This focus means that specialized units are created within the detective division for such crimes as homicide, burglary, auto theft, and so on. The assumption seems to exist that all other requirements of the citizens will be handled by the patrol division. In some departments this may create morale problems because of the misallocation of resources and prestige to the function which is concerned with a minority of police problems.

POLICE ACTION

Under most circumstances the police are dependent upon citizen complaints to alert them to illegal activity. "In a democratic society, the major volume of police work derives from an external source, the citizen complaint, rather than from an internal organizational source, police detection of crimes committed."[15] In this sense the police are primarily reactive, since the typical criminal act occurs at an unpredictable time and in a private rather than a public place. A study of police mobilization in Boston, Chicago, and Washington revealed that 81 percent resulted from citizen telephone calls, 14 percent were initiated in the field by an officer, and 5 percent were requests for service in the field by citizens.[16] Such distribution not only influences the organization of a department, but to a great extent determines the police response to a case.

Police-citizen encounters in situations where the criminal label may be applied are structured by the roles played by each participant, the setting, and the attitudes of the victim toward legal action. The President's Commission found that in only about half the cases of victimization did the victim report the offense. Most often the police were not called because of the belief that they could not or would not do anything. In other incidents the relationship of the offender to the victim discouraged reporting.[17] Studies have shown that the accessibility of the police to the citizen, the complainant's demeanor and characteristics, and the type of violation structure official reaction and the probability of arrest.[18]

All of the foregoing is not to say that the police do not employ proactive strategies, relying on surveillance and undercover work to obtain the required information. But this occurs only in connection with specific types of offenses. Here again, the lack of a complainant forces the police to use informers, "stake-outs," wiretapping, and raids. For those offenses known as "crimes without victims," in which society rather than an individual is supposedly the offended party, proactive tactics are used. This means that the morals and narcotics squads are the primary users of such tactics.

Citing the curbs placed on many police tactics by the Supreme Court, some departments have shifted from an emphasis on enforcing the law to that of reducing crime. Through the use of the proactive tactic of "aggressive patrol" some large cities have developed specially trained squads which are sent to high crime areas to "show the flag." This strategy is also based on the assumption that the public rates the police with reference to the crime rate and that few people know the conviction rate.[19] But we should remember that the primary focusing of police energy springs from the reactive nature of the organization. Black draws the conclusion that because the police rely upon citizens for information concerning law violations, citizens can influence police activity in their neighborhoods.

"To the extent that a police department has an organized dependence upon citizens for ascertaining how its distribution of manpower is to be patterned by localities within a city, the citizens of a given locale unwittingly determine how many policemen will be assigned to their area."[20]

As shown in Figure III-1, Wilson combined the types of legal situations with the basis of the police response to designate the offenses which are found in each category. Each type of case offers a different degree of discretion to the law officials involved, and each type has a different probability of being cleared through some type of formal action.

In police-citizen encounters, problems of fairness to the individual are often intertwined with problems of departmental

Basis of Police Response

Nature of Situation	Police-Invoked		Citizen-Invoked	
Law Enforcement	I.	Crimes without victims	II.	Crimes against persons, property
Order Maintenance	III.	Drunkenness, disorderly conduct	IV.	Calls for assistance— public disorder

Figure III-1.

SOURCE: Adapted from James Q. Wilson, *Varieties of Police Behavior* (Cambridge: Harvard University Press, 1968): 85-89.

policy. When should the patrolman stop and frisk? When should deals be made with the addict-informer? What disputes should be mediated on the spot and which left to adjudicatory personnel?

"The surprising fact is . . . that these mixed problems of justice and policy are seldom decided by heads of departments but are left largely to the discretion of individual policemen, who often act illegally without disapproval of their superiors."[21]

Policemen, then, are what Lipsky has called "street level bureaucrats," since their encounters with citizens allow for extensive independence.[22] In addition, they are primarily concerned with order maintenance situations where the law is not "cut and dried" and where the citizens are often hostile. Because of the situational environment patrolmen must mobilize information quickly, making decisions through the tactics of simplification and routinization where perceptions of the client are based on prior cases. Such a process is likely to lead to error.

The clearance rate, that percentage of crimes known to the police which they believe they have "solved" through an arrest, differs with each category of offense. In those reactive situations such as burglary, the rate of apprehension is extremely low, only about 22 percent. Much greater success of arrest is experienced with violent crimes (59 percent), where the victims tend to know their assailants. Arrests made through proactive police operations against prostitution, gambling, and narcotics have a clearance rate, theoretically, of 100 percent.[23]

The arrest of a person often results in the clearance of other reported offenses, since a major element of police practice is "to utilize the arrested person and knowledge of his current offense as a means of clearing other crimes."[24] Interrogation and line-ups are standard practices, as well as the lesser-known operation of simply assigning unsolved crimes to the defendant in the department's records. Acknowledgment by the offender that he committed prior but unsolved crimes is often part of the bargain when a guilty plea is entered. Professional thieves know that they can gain favors from the police in exchange for "confessing" to those unsolved crimes which they may or may not have committed.[25]

Since the clearance rate is used as a measure of police effectiveness, various strategies are employed to insure that the department and the individual officer look good. It is known that arrest quotas are often used by police administrators as a mechanism of quality control. This practice is most often found in traffic details or in other proactive situations. In other areas these measures may have the effect of persuading the officer to handle a complaint in an informal manner so that his efficiency will not be affected. By urging the complainant not to press charges, making it difficult for witnesses to be found, or by minimizing the offense to his superiors, the patrolman may remove potentially difficult cases so that his effectiveness rating will not be hurt.

POLICE CULTURE

The position of "policeman" is more than a cluster of formally prescribed duties and role expectations held jointly by criminal justice officials and members of the community. In addition to the administrative language of "job specification," "span of control," and "line vs. staff," there is a cultural dimension to the position which has a profound influence on the operational code of the police both as a unit and as individuals behaving within a bureaucratic framework. Since the police, like other low-status occupational groups, have not developed a professional code such as that of lawyers—which emphasizes honor, certification, and internal controls—group norms, situational factors, and culture are important influences. If attention is focused solely upon the legal and formal dimensions of the policeman's role, we may miss the impact of social forces on behavior.

As noted above, discretion is a characteristic of bureaucracy, and within the police bureaucracy discretion has a special dimension: it increases as one moves *down* the hierarchy. Thus, the patrolman, the most numerous and lowest-ranking officer, has the greatest amount of discretion. He deals with clients in isolation, and is in charge of enforcing laws of high ambiguity— conflicts among citizens where the definition of offensive behavior is often open to dispute. His perception of a situation is the crucial determinant of the action to be taken. Wilson has caught the essence of the patrolman's "lot":

> "That role which is unlike that of any other occupation, can be described as one in which sub-professionals, working alone, exercise wide discretion in matters of utmost importance (life and death, honor and dishonor) in an environment that is apprehensive and perhaps hostile."[26]

Social scientists have demonstrated that there is a decided relationship between one's occupational environment and the way events are interpreted;[27] an occupation may be seen as a major badge of identity which a man acts to protect as a facet of his self-esteem and person. As Skolnick has shown, the policeman's "working personality" is distinctive to his occupational group.[28] Because his role contains two important variables, danger and authority, he develops a distinctive cognitive lens through which he views the world. In a similar vein,

> "Entry requirements, training, on- and off-duty behavioral standards, and operational exigencies and goals combine to produce a

homogeneity of attitudes, values and life ways such that members of police forces constitute a distinct subculture within their societies."[29]

These two primary factors, then, "working personality" and culture are so interlocked that they reinforce each other. Thus the daily work of the police is greatly influenced by forces other than those of the organizational structure of law enforcement.

National studies of occupational status have shown that the public ascribes more prestige to the police than in prior decades, yet policemen do not believe that the public regards their calling as honorable. Westley's data (see Table III-1) emphasize the way that policemen think the public views their occupation. Although they are expected to offer assistance with efficiency in times of crisis, they are still often regarded with suspicion, probably because of the fact they must "discipline those whom they serve" and are given the authority to use force to insure compliance.[31]

Throughout the publications of police organizations the theme is repeated that the public does not appreciate and, in fact, is extremely critical of law enforcement agents. In a Denver study officers provided evidence to support their stand that the public did not respect them. Ninety-eight percent reported that they had experienced verbal or physical abuse from the public, and that these incidents tended to occur in neighborhoods of minority and underprivileged groups.[32] Part of the burden of being a policeman is that he is beset with

TABLE III-1

POLICEMAN'S CONCEPTION OF THE PUBLIC'S ATTITUDE
TOWARD THE POLICE

Presumed Public Attitude	Frequency	Percentage
Against the police, hates the police	62	73
Some are for us, some against us	12	13
Likes the police	11	12
Total	85	98

SOURCE: William A. Westley, *Violence and the Police* (Cambridge: MIT Press, 1970): 93.

doubt about his professional status in the public mind. Yet opinion polls consistently indicate that the overwhelming majority of citizens, even those in the ghetto, see the police as protectors of persons and property.

As in few other callings, the policeman's world is circumscribed by the all-encompassing demands of his job. Not only is he socialized to norms which accentuate loyalty to fellow officers, professional esprit de corps, and the symbolism of authority, but the situational context of his position limits his freedom to isolate his vocational role from other aspects of his life. From the time that he is first given his badge and gun, the policeman must always carry these reminders of his position—the tools of his trade—and be prepared to use them. Thus the requirements that he maintain a vigilance against crime even when off-duty and that he work at "odd hours," and his limited opportunities for social contact with persons other than fellow officers reinforce the values of the police subculture.

Although the police bureaucracy allocates duties among officers on the basis of rank and abilities, the police culture overrides these differentiations. Bordua and Reiss believe that this results from the practice of promoting from within.[33] Since there are few opportunities for "lateral entry" into supervisory positions, all members begin at the rank of patrolman. Subsequent upward movement is dependent upon the recommendations of supervisors, with the result that adherence to the occupational culture is strengthened.

Recruitment and Socialization

Recruitment policies are often cited to explain police behavior. Paralleling the rise in crime have been vocal charges by the poor and minority groups that the police use unnecessary physical force in their relations with civilians. It has been said that persons with sadistic or authoritarian tendencies are attracted to police work and are able to secure positions because of the low entry qualifications. Since most communities require only minimal education and experience of those becoming policemen, the belief persists that they do not have the sensitivity necessary to enforce the law amid the social conflicts of the contemporary urban area.

It is true that with few exceptions a high school education, good physical condition, and the absence of a criminal record are all that is necessary to enter police work. In fact, the last requirement is given as the reason police have been unable to recruit residents of the ghetto, where the probability of having had some brush with the law is much higher than in the suburbs. Wilson found that the minimum qualifications varied with the type of department.[34] Those adhering to the "watchman style" stipulated only a bare amount of formal police training, and less than a high school education, while 40 percent of the force in the "service style" community were men with some college background. In a city with a well-entrenched political machine, such as Albany, party work is important both for entry and for promotion.

In pursuit of professionalism efforts have been made to raise educational qualifications and to institute more extensive training. Special programs have been developed in colleges to offer courses in police science toward the goal of securing recruits with at least two years of higher education. Although the educational level of the police has risen over the past fifty years, that of the general population has risen faster.[35] In a department with standards high above the national average such as New York City, only about 15 percent of the applicants pass the screening devices and are accepted into the force. Unfortunately the professionalized departments are few. A 1961 survey by the International Association of Chief of Police showed that of the 243 city departments responding, 24 percent had no educational requirements, and one-third offered two weeks or less of recruit training.[36]

Policemen are recruited from the lower-middle and upper-lower classes of the community. Often there are ethnic and family ties to the local force such that new members are more easily socialized into the norms of the system. McNamara's study of New York showed that although recruits considered their new employment a step up the social ladder, they believed that in relation to other careers, theirs was ascribed low prestige by the general population. In addition, tests showed that they had difficulty separating their police role from personal attitudes in enforcement situations. The feeling that the police were legally "handcuffed" and prevented from carrying out their work was general and grew stronger through the period of formal training. Recruitment of persons from similar backgrounds, together with the status uncertainties of police work, intensifies solidarity within the ranks so that socialization to the code of the "system" is more easily achieved.

Studies of police recruits demonstrate that they hold social attitudes which are typical of their working-class origins: respect for authority and approval of the existing socio-cultural codes of American society. However, regarding political predispositions, Bayley and Mendelsohn found that policemen tend to be more conservative than both the community as a whole and those from their own social strata. In Denver, the site of the study, Goldwater outpolled Johnson among the police in 1964, whereas the winner carried the city almost two to one.[37] Heussenstamm illustrated the influence of political attitudes on police behavior: onto the car bumpers of fifteen students with exemplary driving records, she pasted a brightly colored sticker featuring the slogan "Support The Black Panthers"; the drivers received 33 traffic citations in 17 days.[38]

Police attitudes may possibly be explained by the fact that the job attracts conservatively oriented persons, and that being a policeman intensifies this propensity.

> "The policeman is, by the nature of his calling a defender of the status quo. His job is not to lead social revolutions or to militate for new laws. A person interested in vigorous social innovation would hardly adopt police work as a career. A policeman has a vested interest in maintaining uninterrupted and unimpeded the routine of community life, and he accomplishes this by enforcing existing laws."[39]

In contrast to the charge that policemen tend to be authoritarian, Niederhoffer found that they do not score particularly high on this variable. Of interest is that many who apply for law enforcement positions concurrently seek other civic jobs such as fireman. The attraction of police work does not seem to be so much the opportunity to exert authority and handle a gun, but rather to obtain the security and relatively high economic benefits of a government sinecure. If authoritarianism is a characteristic of the policeman, it is a result of his work situation and socialization rather than a predisposition held by those at the entry level. As Niederhoffer says:

"The police occupational system is geared to manufacture the "take charge guy," and it succeeds in doing so with outstanding efficiency. It is the police system, not the personality of the candidate, that is the more powerful determinant of behavior and ideology."[40]

Although recruits attending the police academy may be taught to respect the civil rights of suspects, the new patrolman is quickly socialized to the realities of police work as defined by his cohorts.

Situational Factors

What are these factors which seem to have such an impact on the "policeman's lot?" Skolnick believes that the role contains the principal variables of danger and authority.[41] There are also subsidiary features such as social isolation and secrecy which influence behavior. As the member of a craft, the policeman is unable to refer to a generalized body of theory of written knowledge. Apprenticeship is on the job and respect comes from colleagues. However, unlike other craftsmen, "the police work in an apprehensive or hostile environment producing a service the value of which is not easily judged."[42]

The danger of his role makes the policeman especially attentive to signs indicating a potential for violence and lawbreaking. Throughout his socialization he is reminded of incautious actions and is told stories about fellow officers killed by assailants when they were not on their guard. Thus, the policeman becomes a "suspicious" person, paying particular regard to anyone and any situation which does not fit his perceptions of normalcy. It is here that the cultural values of the police come to the fore. The greater the departure from the officer's conception of the middle-class norm, the greater his suspicion of the subject.[43] A black man running through a white suburb late at night, even though wearing a track suit, may be perceived as a fleeing burglar. In fact, Chevigney believes that the mere presence of members of outcast groups is seen as an affront to order, such that the police will themselves initiate action by ordering such persons to move along, by breaking into a party, or by some similar action.

The element of unexpected danger in his work creates tension in the policeman; he is constantly "on edge" and worried about the possibility of attack. This is sensed by those he stops for questioning. The suspect may not intend to attack the officer, yet he feels what he believes to be an unnecessary hostility. "If the citizen shows his resentment, the officer is likely to interpret it as animosity and thus to be even more on his guard."[44] Because his work requires him to be continually preoccupied with potential violence, the policeman "develops a perceptual shorthand to identify certain kinds of people as symbolic assailants ... persons who use gestures, language, and attire that the policeman has come to recognize as a prelude to violence"[45] —long hair, motorcycle jackets, "jiving," and loitering, for example.

The policeman represents authority and is thus always in the position of being challenged. But, as Westley explains,

> "there is something about the occupation and social position of the police that engenders a feeling on the policeman's part that no one respects his authority and that he has to maintain such respect."[46]

The authority factor, although as important as the element of danger in the situational context of the policeman's life, is much more complex since its influence relates to the concepts of self-esteem and secrecy.

As distinguished from the detective, the patrolman is primarily concerned with the maintenance of order, an area of the law where there may be a great deal of disagreement among citizens. As we have noted, order-maintenance requires that he stop fights, arrest drunks, and settle domestic quarrels—circumstances in which the citizen is not at his best, the pertinent laws are inexact, and the presence of an officer may not be welcome. And, moreover, circumstances which require the patrolman to "handle the situation" rather than enforce the law; to assert his authority without becoming personally involved. Further, he must regulate a public which "denies recognition of his authority and stresses his obligation to respond to danger."[47]

The citizen may challenge the policeman's authority by charging him with hypocrisy regarding his personal conduct, making insinuations about his manhood, and in general deprecating his right to enforce the law. Such verbal aggression is a major ingredient in the policeman's role, yet he is expected to respond in a detached or neutral manner.

The policeman is a symbol of authority whose occupational prestige may be defined as low, yet at times he must give orders to those with status. As Westley explains:

"He expects rage from the underprivileged and the criminal but understanding from the middle classes: the professionals, the merchants, and the white collar workers. They, however define him as a servant, not a colleague, and the rejection is hard to take"[48]

Given the working-class background of the "cop," the maintenance of self-respect, the proving of masculinity, and the refusal to take "crap" may be important ways by which he deals with the problem of authority. A major emphasis of police work is the need to assert authority upon arriving at the scene when arrival itself may generate hostility. This may lead to the use of excessive force or violence by a policeman who feels that his authority has been put into question by a person who presents a danger to the officer and the community. Cries of "police brutality" often spring from such a circular chain of events.

In one of the first sociological studies of law enforcement, Westley describes the links among the norms of secrecy, violence, and the social isolation of the police. As he points out, "Where they have respect from the public, they will have less need for violence and secrecy. Where public hostility grows, so will their utilization of violence and secrecy." These concepts further define and link the authority and danger factors in the situational influence on police behavior. Since the police view the public as hostile, they tend to isolate themselves, developing strong in-group attitudes which demand that the individual officer conform to group norms. Also, distrust of outsiders develops almost to the point of paranoia, so that secrecy stands as a shield against attacks from the outside world.

> "Secrecy is loyalty, for it represents sticking with the group, and its maintenance carries with it a profound sense of participation. Secrecy is solidarity, for it represents a common front against the outside world and consensus in at least one goal."[49]

In a peculiar twist, police solidarity may be used to cover their illegal activities. Tales of stationhouse justice are well known, but secrecy may also shield false arrests, perjury, and prejudice. Early in his training the rookie is impressed with the first rules of the police culture: "Keep your mouth shut, never squeal on a fellow officer, and don't be a stool pigeon."

The situational influences on the policeman, plus the conditions under which he is recruited and socialized, have a direct effect on his law enforcement practices. As a result, the patrolman may find that he is on safe ground when he follows routines and does not "stick his neck out." Wilson and Banton feel that in ordinary matters the organizational consequence is for patrolmen to underenforce the law.[50]

POLICE-COMMUNITY RELATIONS

Since the long, hot summers of the late 1960's, increased attention has been focused on the relationship of the police to the urban (especially black) community. It is at this level where the daily interactions between the citizen and police occur, that the factors discussed previously concerning the nature of the law enforcement function, police culture, recruitment and socialization form a constellation, accentuated by the social environment of the urban community, which together create a potential for explosions. It is one thing to speak of the police role in a small, homogeneous town where there is consensus on which values the police shall enforce and another thing to speak

of that role in the entirely different context of the heterogeneous urban environment. To expect a white, suburban-based
patrolman of working-class background to maintain order in
Harlem would do him and Harlem a disservice.

With the migration of the white middle class from the inner
city, its place has been taken by blacks, Puerto Ricans, the
young, and the aged. In addition, there remain those working-
class whites who feel trapped by their inability to accumulate
the means to follow their brothers to the suburbs. It is hard to
imagine a more heterogeneous assemblage; the potential for
conflict could not be higher.

The physical context of the inner city heightens the social
friction. As Wilson has told us, personal and family privacy is at
a premium—the street is often where the resident conducts
many of his social interactions.[51] This makes his trans-
gressions more visible. Rather than gambling in a den or game
room, the slum dweller uses the sidewalk. Family quarrels are in
the open for all to hear. Older white couples living in apartment
buildings with large black families complain of noise. All of
these conditions contribute to the order-maintenance role of
the police.

For many persons, the police officer is their only contact
with government. The way he does his work has an impact on
the citizen's view of justice in the political system. By
conceptualizing justice as the "congruence between expectations about key officials in the justice system and perceptions
of the actual behavior," Jacob studiesd attitudes toward the
police in a variety of Milwaukee neighborhoods.[52] A portion
of his data, shown in Table III-2, indicates that blacks perceive
the police as more corrupt, more unfair, tougher, and excitable
than do respondents in the white neighborhoods. However,
Jacob found that race is not the sole variable, since some blacks
viewed the police in the same light as whites. Rather race and
personal experience with the police "may interact with each
other to produce different results in several neighborhoods."[53]

The President's Commission has stated that permissive law
enforcement and police brutality are the two basic reasons for

TABLE III-2

PERCEPTIONS OF ACTUAL POLICE: MEAN SCORES IN THREE
NEIGHBORHOOD SAMPLES

Scales	Ghetto	White Working Class	White Middle Class
(1 ... Score ... 7)	(n=71)	(n=71)	(n=73)
Honest ... Corrupt	3.30	2.25	1.84
Bad ... Good	4.10	6.04	6.10
Unfair ... Fair	3.76	5.56	6.03
Excitable ... Calm	3.42	5.69	4.97
Lazy ... Hardworking	4.62	5.86	5.85
Smart ... Dumb	2.76	1.93	2.02
Friendly ... Unfriendly	3.63	2.06	2.08
Kind ... Cruel	3.82	2.14	2.10
Strong ... Weak	2.66	2.04	2.12
Harsh ... Easygoing	3.04	3.86	3.68
Tough ... Softhearted	2.49	3.24	2.70

SOURCE: Adapted from: Herbert Jacob, "Black and White Perceptions of Justice in
the City," paper presented at the Sixty-Sixth Annual Meetings of the American
Political Science Association, Los Angeles, September 8-12, 1970: 3.

resentment by residents of the urban community.[54] The
police are charged with failure to give adequate protection and
services in minority group neighborhoods, and with using
physical or verbal abuse in their contacts with residents. In a
study of New York's Bedford-Stuyvesant area, respondents
listed eight factors of conflict and antagonism with the police:
abrasive relationships between the police and black juveniles,
police toleration of narcotics traffic, the small number of black
patrolmen stationed in black neighborhoods, inefficient handling of emergencies, lack of respect toward black citizens, low
police morale, not enough patrolmen, and inadequate patrol in
black neighborhoods.[55]

Uneven law enforcement has long been a complaint of
minority groups. A survey of Harlem in 1964 showed that 39
percent of those interviewed considered "crime and criminals"
as the biggest problem for Negroes in the area. The belief exists
that when an incident occurs among members of the same
group, the police treat violations more lightly than when
members of different groups are involved. In a hostile environment the white patrolman may fear that breaking up a street

fight will only provoke the wrath of onlookers. Cultural traits
are also given by the police as a reason for not enforcing the
law—"Those people live like that, it's in their nature." As a
participant-observer on New York's West Side, Lyford found
that residents felt that the police exert themselves only for
crimes such as murder or assault, or where matters can be
disposed of neatly (parking violations). They do not work
effectively on the in-between crimes such as narcotics, gambling, petty thievery, or in-group assault. "These are the crimes
that flood the area and cause the insecurity and fear."[56]
Because they do not stringently enforce morals statutes, police
are believed by residents to be paid off and, accordingly, to be
no better than criminals.

We have already noted the way police stereotype citizens.
Practically all studies document prejudicial attitudes of policemen toward blacks. Reiss found that a majority of white
officers in Boston, Chicago, and Washington held anti-Negro
attitudes.

> "In the predominantly Negro precincts, over three-fourths of the
> white policemen expressed prejudiced or highly prejudiced senti-
> ments towards members of the Negro race."[57]

These attitudes, together with the stereotyping mechanism, lead
many policemen to view all blacks as slum dwellers and thus
potential criminals, and this results in their exaggerating the
extent of black crime. Kephart found that although Negroes
comprised about 70 percent of all persons arrested, white
officers of the Philadelphia force estimated that the average was
over 95 percent.[58] There is little wonder that the ghetto
resident thinks of the police as an army of occupation and that
the police think of themselves as combat soldiers.

One of the great disparities in American criminal justice is the
absence of black policemen. Many authorities assume that they
would have easier relations with inner-city residents and be
more sympathetic to their needs. It has been estimated that of
the 80,000 sworn personnel in twenty-eight major cities, only
7,000 are nonwhite. Surveys have shown that in no major
American city does the police force approximate the ratio of

Negroes in the community. For example, in Baltimore, where nonwhites comprise 41 percent of the population, only 7 percent of the policemen are nonwhite. At the officer and policy-making levels the disparities increase.

A failure of recent years has been the effort to recruit more blacks into urban police forces. Only the District of Columbia has had any degree of success. Part of the failure has been attributed to the fact that many departments have not been aggressive enough in their search. On the other hand, some observers believe that the ghetto-held stereotype of the policeman does not inspire emulation. A stronger factor is probably the prejudice existing within departments which often means that black policemen are assigned to the dirty jobs, must suffer from the racial slurs of their fellow officers, and endure conflicting feelings toward members of the black community which they are asked to patrol.[59]

Police Brutality

The rising voices of excluded groups have brought incidents of police brutality into the open. Although the poor have suffered these indignities for generations, it has been only recently that a wakened public has focused attention on the illegal use of violence by the police. More citizens are aware of their rights and are prepared to defend their rights at a time when the political system is more vulnerable to complaints. The actions of the Chicago police during the 1968 Democratic National Convention brought forth a government report, *Rights in Conflict,* which illustrated to middle-class Americans a view of the police which they never knew. A study for the President's Commission conducted by Reiss found that "police brutality" is used to cover a wide variety of actions all the way from discourtesy to violence. He notes:

"What citizens object to and call 'police brutality' is really the judgment that they have not been treated with the full rights and dignity owing citizens in a democratic society."[60]

We can never know the amount of force used illegally

because of the low visibility of police-citizen interactions and the reluctance of victims to file charges against their assailants. Policemen are authorized by law to use necessary force to make arrests, yet there is no agreement on the amount of force necessary. Is it better to let the suspect escape than to employ "deadly" force? Although the popular impression casts police brutality as a racial matter, Reiss found that white suspects are liable to be treated more improperly than are Negro suspects. He believes that in fact it is surprising that there is not a greater amount of police brutality, yet forty-four citizens were improperly assaulted by police in Boston, Chicago, and Washington before the eyes of Reiss's observers during the summer of 1966.

Following a two-year study of police practices in New York City, Chevigney concluded that it is virtually impossible to bring men to task for unprofessional behavior. Through a variety of ways the police are usually able to camouflage misconduct so that victims are unable to secure redress. If a false arrest is made, there is a great temptation for police to charge *something* against the citizen to avoid the negative consequences of a suit or the disfavor of superiors. In instances of physical abuse, the lack of witnesses, the code of secrecy, and the powerlessness of the victim prevent the disciplining of the abuser. Chevigney documents incidents which can only lessen respect for the law, noting, "There is no more embittering experience in the legal system than to be abused by the police and then to be tried and convicted on false evidence."[61]

We have already seen that many police actions occur in situations of low visibility. The back seat of the squad car and the inner recesses of the stationhouse are areas relatively safe from observation. Furthermore, there is a tendency for citizens to avoid becoming involved. Attempts to bring formal charges against the police are often frustrated by the lack of witnesses. In addition, Chevigney reports that the courts are reluctant to give credence to civilian complainants, since to impeach a policeman may be viewed as an assault against the entire criminal justice system.[62]

The code of brotherhood and secrecy among the police has

been documented by Westley.[63] He found that eleven out of fifteen men said that they would not report a brother officer for taking money from a prisoner, and ten out of thirteen said they would not testify against the officer if he were accused by the prisoner. Policemen will lie to protect themselves and each other. This is justified within the department by the fraternal bond and the fear of outsiders.

Throughout their socialization policemen are reminded of the potential for civil suit on the charge of false arrest. This is usually the only course open to the citizen and presents an interesting paradox. The suit is against an individual officer, yet he may be following departmental policy. Reiss and Bordua make clear the implications of this situation. "If affecting the department's mission lays the officer open to suit, clearly a norm of secrecy and mutual support is a highly likely result."[64]

To insure that false arrest suits are not brought against the police, law enforcement officers use "cover charges"—such as disorderly conduct, resisting arrest, and assault—to protect themselves. Each of these charges is designed to account for an action by the police. The disorderly conduct charge accounts for the arrest, while the others may be used if the defendant has been injured or otherwise physically abused. Still other charges may be included to increase the bargaining power of the police, thus insuring that the victim will agree to exonerate the officer from the threat of suit. The charges stand in the way of obtaining redress. If one is unable to get acquitted on the cover charges, there is no point in complaining about police brutality. In order to have the charges dismissed the prosecutor often requests that the defendant sign a waiver of damage claims against the city and the individual officer. This is often too tempting a bargain for most victims to pass up. Refusal to agree to the conditions of the waiver will almost certainly bring the expense and uncertainty of a trial.

From direct observation in the precincts, investigators for the President's Commission found that officers at the middle level of the organization tend to cover the misdeeds of men working directly below them.[65] This is characteristic of police solidarity, and also enables a sergeant to hold the threat of exposure over his patrolmen.

Those victims of brutality or false arrest who feel strong enough about their cause to register a formal complaint or to bring civil suit have great difficulty. In one eastern city the department used to charge citizens who complained of police misconduct with filing false reports.[66] In Philadelphia the police review board found that it seemed to be standard practice to charge a person with resisting arrest or disorderly conduct whenever that person accused the police of brutality.[67]

In recent years there have been attempts to develop greater citizen control over police affairs. The creation of civilian review boards or the inclusion of outsiders as participants in disciplinary hearings have been tried in a number of cities. The record is dismal. During the seven-year period, 1958-1965, the Philadelphia Civilian Review Board processed 704 complaints, but recommended penalties against the policemen involved in only thirty-eight cases.[68] In New York voters defeated a review board by a two-to-one margin following a bitter campaign with charges by the police that the proponents were coddling criminals. Wilson may be correct when he points out that review boards will not affect substantive police policies since behavior objected to results more from

"styles created by general organizational arrangements and departmental attitudes and partly because grievances procedures deal with specific complaints about unique circumstances, not with general practices of the officers."[69]

As Levine reminds us, the victims of police brutality are ordinarily marginal, lower-class men who lack the initiative, resources, and skills to fight the injustices inflicted upon them. These kinds of persons have a low sense of political efficacy regarding legal institutions and are either unaware of the channels open to them or dubious of their chances for success.

"Thus we have the paradox that those who hate the police the most, the racial minorities in the ghettos, took less advantage of the presumably responsive Civilian Review Board in New York during its short existence than the middle-class whites. If those who suffer most complain the least, guilty police are not likely to apprehended."[70]

POLICE AND THE ADMINISTRATION OF JUSTICE

As has been emphasized before, the system of criminal justice is composed of many units, or subsystems, which are intricately linked in a complex of relationships. This is consistent with the idea of Reiss and Bordua, who say:

"The legal system is not a seamless web of tightly articulated rules and roles ... but a loose-jointed system held together at many points by micro-systems of antagonistic cooperation and discretionary decisions."[71]

In the justice system the police stand as the essential gateway for the entrance of the raw materials to be processed. The cases which are sent to the prosecutor for charging, and thence to the courts for adjudication, have their beginning with the decision of an individual police officer that probable cause exists to effect an arrest. Unlike most other systems of formal organization, the administration of criminal justice is characterized by the fact that the ultimate fate of clients rests in another group of clients. Decisions made by the police concerning offenders may be reversed by the prosecutor or judge. Although the police may introduce clients into the system through their power of arrest, assessment of the outcome of a case is in the hands of the prosecutor and court. Police do have final power in those cases filtered out of the system at the intake point.

In addition to exchange relationships among persons in the criminal justice system, police decisions are also influenced by other governmental agencies, interest groups, and community elites. This penetration of the police organizational environment results both from the overlapping jurisdictions of county, state, and national law enforcement agencies and political context of criminal justice decisions.

In his study of traffic enforcement in four Massachusetts

towns, Gardiner found that city officials with budgetary powers, individual citizens, and groups such as the safety council all tried to insist that the police follow *their* perceptions of the way the law should be enforced.[72] Attempts to "fix" tickets through the intervention of politicians or police officials in other communities were found to be common. Massachusetts police chiefs believe that traffic enforcement can jeopardize public relations more than any other phase of their work. If ticket-writing campaigns are too active, they fear for their budget and community support. Traffic policy-making must be carried out in a context of sporadic citizen demands and group pressures, so that policy results from "vague picking and choosing among public values."[73]

Many of the exchange relationships between the police and their clientele are cooperative. The extensive communications network between the Federal Bureau of Investigation and local police forces is a good example. The FBI performs important and helpful services for the local agencies by publicizing the names of wanted criminals, providing background information on offenders, and completing technical operations such as fingerprint analysis for those departments lacking such expertise. At the same time there are organizational and political benefits to be gained by the FBI. In the name of the coordinated effort against crime, law enforcement agencies at the national and state levels have developed important clientele relationships. Presumably the political support of local officials is the payment which is made for the services rendered.[74]

Within the criminal justice system the police have a peculiar relationship to the prosecution and judicial subsystems. Although the police have the power to introduce clients into the larger system, they are formally required to allow other agencies to evaluate their work product. The traditional index of police effectiveness has been the number of arrests rather than either the number of convictions or the nature of the sentences imposed. Toward this end they may be primarily moved to generate "information that links a person with a criminal event or helps to maintain public order,"[75] and less concerned about the admissibility of evidence or other due process criteria.

Prosecutors may be motivated to insure that the cases brought to them by the police will easily pass the scrutiny of the judge and result in a conviction. They may require that the police develop an exceptional level of evidence in certain cases before they will be willing to act. Since the prosecutor knows that he has more to lose than just the case if the victim refuses to cooperate, if the evidence is skimpy, and if the judge is known to dislike a certain type of case, he may convince the police to handle the offender some other way. The filtering system gives the police discretion to drop cases without the necessity of approval from other judicial units.

Bargaining between the police and court personnel is thus characterized by an inequality and a reversal of roles. When a policeman interrogates a suspected offender he is in a superior position and is able to use tactics which assert his authority in the situation. However, in contacts with the prosecutor and courts, the policeman is below the formal and social status of the officials with whom he must deal. Under trial conditions the officer may even be placed in the position where he himself is interrogated by a member of the bar. In addition, court officers such as probation and juvenile personnel, whose social status may not be as high as that of attorneys or judges, are nonetheless formally superior to the police. As Reiss carefully delineates:

"When the ultimate fate of clients rests in another group of clients—particularly when they are removed from the situation that precipitated the client relationship—conflict is endemic in the system."[76]

In all of the bargaining relationships within the criminal justice bureaucracy, the police must interact with persons who may view law enforcement with hostility. In fact, many are hired because of their adversarial stance toward the police. Yet these exchange relationships are not completely one-sided; the police have sanctions which they too may use in their dealings with the prosecutor and judge. Often these take the form of informal and *sub rosa* practices such as inducing suspects to plead guilty to a host of prior unsolved offenses in return for leniency. Or, if there are questions as to the receptivity of the prosecutor to filing charges, the police may take justice into their own hands and mete out punishment in the stationhouse. Alternatively, the patrolman may simply decide not to arrest.

Arrest and the Filtering Process

As in other areas in the administration of justice, reliable statistics concerning police decision-making are not available. The evidence which is known leaves little doubt that the police use their discretionary powers to filter out those defendants whose cases are not deemed to be worthy, from an organizational perspective, of prosecution. As we have shown above, the low visibility of police decisions allows little public observation and critique of these practices. Very little is known about the characteristics of those defendants whose cases are kept in the system compared to the characteristics of those whose cases are removed. At least one scholar has suggested that these decisions are made primarily on the basis of incentives and sanctions which are present within the administrative context.[77] Our guess is that the poor and minorities are especially disadvantaged by the filtering process, primarily because they are unable to create, through attorneys, the adversarial tension which is used by the well-off to insure proper handling of their cases.

The decision to take a suspect into custody is almost always made by the police on the spot and without a formal arrest warrant. As described earlier in this chapter, this is based on factors such as the officer's personality, departmental policy, his knowledge of the case, and perceptions of the attitudes of other judicial actors, particularly those of the prosecutor. Most often citizens are taken into custody on suspicion, so that there are no grounds as to the legality of the arrest itself. Such arrests also give the police greater freedom to drop the suspect from the system without the need for a complete explanation.

In a study of the felony arrests in California in 1960, Barrett found that 28.5 percent of the 98,921 suspects were released without any charges having been filed in court.[78] An additional 6.6 percent were turned over to other jurisdictions for prosecution, and 21.6 percent had their charges reduced to a misdemeanor. As a result of police decisions during this early stage, 55,994 defendants were removed from the felony process before formal complaints had been filed.

Variations in the filtering process occur in different localities and for different offenses. In California the highest release rate occurred in metropolitan areas, the lowest in rural areas. Based on the charges, release rates varied from a high for robbery (42.6 percent) and aggravated assault (32.2 percent) to a low for forgery and checks (10.3 percent) and sex offenses (17.9 percent). We may speculate about the influence of factors such as caseload pressures in the system and the nature of the police action, either proactive or reactive.

In California the data indicated that police and prosecutors apply different standards "to the decision to arrest than they do to the decision to charge."[79] This means that about one out of every two adults arrested will ultimately be convicted of either a felony or a misdemeanor. When this same measurement is taken at the point where complaints are filed, the ratio increases so that three out of every four charged will be convicted.

It should not be assumed that all police departments filter cases to the extent of those in California. Levin's studies of Pittsburgh and Minneapolis would suggest that the police and prosecutors in those cities give the courts a greater opportunity to remove cases from the system.[80] Yet the other fragmentary evidence which is available and referred to in Chapter II suggests that filtering in California is similar to that found in New York City and Detroit.[81] Further research in this area should be a priority item for social scientists interested in criminal justice.

POLITICS AND THE POLICE

Given the rhetoric about "crime in the streets," police-community relations, and the need for law and order, one would expect a high degree of citizen influence exerted over police decisions so that politics would be a key factor in law enforcement. This is not the case. It appears that the particularistic nature of police work lowers the interest of most citizens. "Police protection is an exceptional service which exists to prevent things from happening. It is largely invisible, and the average citizen comes into contact with it only in the exceptional case."[82] Unlike garbage collection, it is difficult for most citizens to measure the police service which he is receiving. This means that police actions such as brutality, traffic safety crackdowns, and the flagrant operation of vice may bring about a public outcry, but for most people it is "others" who have contact with the law.

There are a number of outstanding examples of the relationship of politics and the police. Circumstances such as those described by Gardiner as existing in "Wincanton," where organized crime had direct links to government officials, political forces are constantly involved in the daily operations of the police.[83] The reaction of the Daley administration to the Walker Commission Report of the police riot in Chicago indicates that political forces felt there were to be gains from a defense of the police. In addition, there have been a number of cities, Minneapolis and Philadelphia for example, where police officials have run for mayor as "law and order" candidates. These are instances where the direct relationship between partisan politics and the police is evident. More important is the fact that law enforcement and the administration of justice encompasses certain political values which are reflected in the way police operations are carried out. As shown above, enforcement policies, the distribution of resources, and the social backgrounds of police officers influence the allocation of values.

In Wilson's examination of the police of eight communities it was discovered that law enforcement activities are governed by the dominant values of the local political culture. As he says, "Police work is carried out under the influence of a political culture though not necessarily under day-to-day political direction."[84] Using this conceptual framework it is difficult to see a direct political involvement in most police operations;

rather the choice of an administrator is a major political decision. Decision makers assume that the chief will run the department in ways which reflect local goals and norms.

The police administrator is a key figure in law enforcement politics, since he links the department to other decision makers, public officials, and community elites. He must operate the department within the context of the political environment according to the expectations of dominant groups. Wilson found three major styles of police operations. Each reflects the socio-political characteristics of the community. These attributes influence the types of arrests and the implementation of law enforcement policies. The "Watchman" style, found in economically declining cities with traditional political machines, emphasizes order maintenance. The "legalistic" style corresponds to cities with heterogeneous populations and a reform-oriented, professional government. Law enforcement of both a reactive and proactive nature characterizes this style. In the homogeneous suburban communities a "service" style, oriented toward the needs of citizens, predominates police activity. In each, the political culture dictates the style so that the police are sensitive to the political environment without being governed by it.

The police are a major ingredient of the larger criminal justice system, yet they have problems which are inherent in their work. Although emphasis is now being placed on up-grading law enforcement through higher education requirements and new equipment, these inducements alone will not solve the problems of the police. Within the justice system the police must be atuned to exchange relationships with a political overtone. They must also be aware of the political and social environment within which law enforcement activities are cast.

NOTES

1. Jerome Hall, "Police and Law in Democratic Society," Indiana Law Journal 28 (Winter, 1953), 162.

2. Abraham S. Blumberg and Arthur Niederhoffer, "The Police in Social and Historical Perspective," *The Ambivalent Force: Perspectives on the Police,* ed. Arthur Niederhoffer and Abraham Blumberg (Waltham: Ginn and Company, 1970), 7.

3. Herbert Packer, *The Limits of the Criminal Sanction* (Stanford: Stanford University Press, 1968).

4. Jerome Skolnick, *Justice Without Trial: Law Enforcement in Democratic Society* (New York: Wiley, 1966), 6.

5. Joseph Goldstein, "Police Discretion Not to Invoke the Criminal Process: Low-Visibility Decisions in the Administration of Justice," Yale Law Journal, 69 (March, 1960), 543-594. Also: Wayne LaFave, "The Police and Nonenforcement of the Law," Wisconsin Law Review (1962), 104-137; 179-239.

6. Emile Durkheim, *The Rules of Sociological Method* (New York: Free Press, 1964), 67. Also: Kai Ericksen, *Wayward Puritans* (New York: Wiley, 1966); Howard Becker, *Outsiders: Studies in the Sociology of Deviance* (New York: Free Press, 1963).

7. President's Commission on Law Enforcement and Administration of Justice, *Task Force Report: The Police,* 15.

8. Blumberg and Niederhoffer, 2.

9. James Q. Wilson, *Varieties of Police Behavior* (Cambridge: Harvard University Press, 1968), 16; Michael Banton, *The Policeman in the Community* (London: Tavistock, 1964), 6-7.

10. Egon Bittner, "The Police on Skid Row: A Study of Peace Keeping," American Sociological Review, 32 (October, 1967), 699-715.

11. Wilson, 17.

12. Elaine Cumming, Ian Cumming, and Laura Edell, "Policeman as Philosopher, Guide and Friend," Social Problems, 12 (1965), 267-286.

13. Thomas E. Bercal, "Calls for Police Assistance: Consumer Demands for Governmental Service," American Behavioral Scientist, 13 (1970), 681-691; Herman Goldstein, "Police Response to Urban Crisis," Public Administration Review (Sept./Oct., 1968), 417-423.

14. Wilson, 69.

15. Albert J. Reiss, Jr., and David J. Bordua, "Environment and Organization: A Perspective on the Police," *The Police: Six Sociological Essays,* ed. David J. Bordua (New York: John Wiley, 1967), 41.

16. Donald J. Black and Albert J. Reiss, Jr., "Patterns of Behavior in Police and Citizen Transactions," President's Commission on Law Enforcement and Administration of Justice, *Studies in Crime and Law Enforcement in Major Metropolitan Areas,* 2, Field Surveys III (1967), 4-5.

17. Philip H. Ennis, "Criminal Victimization in the United States, A Report of a National Survey," President's Commission on Law Enforcement and Administration of Justice, Field Surveys II (1967), 41-51.

18. Black and Reiss, 51-57.

19. Fred Graham, *The Self-Inflicted Wound* (New York: Macmillan, 1970), 141.

20. Donald J. Black, "Police Encounters and Social Organization: An Observational Study" (unpublished Ph.D. dissertation, University of Michigan, 1968), 23.

21. Kenneth C. Davis, *Discretionary Justice* (Baton Rouge: Louisiana State University Press, 1969), 8.

22. Michael Lipsky, "Toward a Theory of Street-Level Bureaucracy," paper presented at the Annual Meetings of the American Political Science Association, 1969.

23. President's Commission, *Task Force Report: The Police,* 188; Donald J. Black, "Production of Crime Rates," American Sociological Review (August, 1970), 735.

24. Reiss and Bordua, 43.

25. Bruce Jackson, *A Thief's Primer* (New York: Macmillan, 1969); Skolnick, 164-181.

26. Wilson, 30.

27. Seymour Martin Lipset, Martin Trow, and James Coleman, *Union Democracy* (New York: Free Press, 1955); Everett C. Hughes, *Men and Their Work* (New York: Free Press, 1958); Alvin W. Gouldner, *Patterns of Industrial Bureaucracy* (New York: Free Press, 1954).

28. Skolnick, 42.

29. Daniel H. Swett, "Cultural Bias in the American Legal System," Law and Society Review, 4 (August, 1969), 79.

30. Paul K. Hatt and C. C. North, "Prestige Ratings of Occupations," Man, Work and Society, ed. Sigmund Nosow and William Form (New York: Basic Books, 1962), 277-283.

31. William Westley, *Violence and the Police* (Cambridge: M.I.T. Press, 1971), 35.

32. Donald Bayley and Harold Mendelsohn, *Minorities and the Police* (New York: Free Press, 1969), 27.

33. David J. Bordua and Albert J. Reiss, Jr., "Command, Control, and Charisma: Reflections on Police Bureaucracy," American Journal of Sociology, 72 (July, 1966), 68-76.

34. Wilson, 151.

35. John H. McNamara, "Uncertainties in Police Work: The Relevance of Police Recruits' Backgrounds and Training," *The Police,* ed. Bordua, 187.

36. Ed Cray, *The Big Blue Line: Police Power vs. Human Rights* (New York: Coward-McCann, 1967), 204.

37. Bayley and Mendelsohn, 18.

38. F. K. Heussenstamm, "Bumper Stickers and The Cops," Transaction, February, 1971, 32-33.

39. Bayley and Mendelsohn, 28.

40. Arthur Niederhoffer, *Behind the Shield* (Garden City: Doubleday, 1967), 151.

41. Skolnick, 42-70.

42. Wilson, 283.

43. Swett, "Cultural Bias in the American Legal System," 93.

44. Wilson, 20.

45. Skolnick, 45.

46. Westley, 8.

47. Skolnick, 45.

48. Westley, 56.

49. *Ibid.,* 111.

50. Wilson, 49; Banton, 127-136.

51. James Q. Wilson, "The Police and Their Problems: A Theory," Public Policy, 12 (1963), 189-216. See also Michael Banton, *The Policeman in the Community* (New York: Basic Books, 1964).

52. Herbert Jacob, "Black and White Perceptions of Justice in the City," paper

presented at the Annual Meetings of the American Political Science Association, 1970.

53. Ibid.

54. "A National Survey of Police and Community Relations," President's Commission on Law Enforcement and Administration of Justice, Field Surveys V, 1967, 14.

55. Ibid., 15.

56. Joseph P. Lyford, *The Airtight Cage* (New York: Harper and Row, 1966), 294.

57. Albert J. Reiss, Jr., "Police Brutality–Answers to Key Questions," Transaction, July-August, 1968, 10-19.

58. William Kephart, *Racial Factors in Urban Law Enforcement* (Philadelphia: University of Pennsylvania, 1957); Westley, *Violence and the Police*, 99.

59. New York Times, September 28, 1969. Also: Robert Conot, *Rivers of Blood, Years of Darkness* (New York: Morrow, 1968), for examples of prejudice within the Los Angeles department.

60. Reiss, "Police Brutality," 12. Also: Herman Goldstein, "Administrative Problems in Controlling the Exercise of Police Authority," Journal of Criminal Law, Criminology and Police Science, 58 (June, 1967), 160-172.

61. Paul Chevigney, *Police Power* (New York: Vintage, 1969), 283.

62. Ibid., 141.

63. Westley, 113-114.

64. Reiss and Bordua, 39. Also: Wayne LaFave, *Arrest: The Decision to Take a Suspect into Custody* (Boston: Little Brown, 1965).

65. President's Commission, Field Surveys V, 189.

66. Chevigney, 48-49; LaFave, *Arrest*, 411-417.

67. President's Commission, *Task Force Report: The Police*, 195.

68. *Ibid.* See also: Algernon Black, *The People and the Police* (New York: McGraw Hill, 1968).

69. Wilson, 229.

70. James Levine, "Implementing Legal Policies Through Operant Conditioning: The Case of Police Practices," paper presented at the Annual Meetings of the American Political Science Association, 1970, 19.

71. Reiss and Bordua, 26.

72. John Gardiner, *Traffic and the Police: Variations in Law Enforcement Policy* (Cambridge: Harvard University Press, 1969), 116.

73. Ibid., 117.

74. Aaron Wildavsky, *The Politics of the Budgetary Process* (Boston: Little Brown, 1964).

75. Albert Reiss and Donald J. Black, "Interrogation and the Criminal Process," Annals, 374 (1967), 52.

76. Albert Reiss, "The Role of the Police in a Changing Society," Working Papers of the Center for Research on Social Organization, 14 (March, 1966), 15.

77. William Chambliss, *Crime and the Legal Process* (New York: McGraw-Hill, 1969), 86.

78. Edward L. Barrett, Jr., "Police Practices and the Law–From Arrest to Release or Charge," California Law Review, 50 (1962), 31-35.

79. Ibid., 34.

80. Martin A. Levin, "Urban Political Systems and Judicial Behavior: The

Criminal Courts in Minneapolis and Pittsburgh" (unpublished Ph.D. dissertation, Department of Government, Harvard University, 1970).

81. Nathan R. Sobel, "Crime in New York City," Brooklyn Law Review, 30 (1963), 13; President's Commission, *Task Force Report: The Courts,* 130.

82. Wilson, 235.

83. John Gardiner, "Wincanton: The Politics of Corruption," President's Commission on Law Enforcement and Administration of Justice, *Task Force Report: Organized Crime,* 61-79.

84. Wilson, 233.

PROSECUTING

ATTORNEY*

"Nowhere is it more apparent that our government is a government of men, not of laws. Nowhere do the very human elements of dishonesty, ambition, greed, lust for power, laxness or bigotry have more room for development. Also, there is no office where an able and honest public servant can be more effective."[1]

The fearless prosecuting attorney,[2] overcoming political pressures as he fights crime and seeks to maintain order, is an American folk hero. The image of the sheriff as the power of the law in frontier America may be compared to that of the prosecutor in our increasingly urbanized environment. Through novels, motion pictures, and television the glamour of the prosecuting attorney's role has been presented to the public.

The crusading prosecutors of fiction have their counterparts in political life. One can readily bring to mind such recent

*This chapter is based on the author's Ph.D. dissertation, "The Politics of Prosecution: The Decision to Prosecute" (University of Washington, 1968). Unless otherwise noted, quotations are from the respondents to that study, an examination of the Office of Prosecuting Attorney in King County (Seattle) and Skagit County, Washington.

public figures as Earl Warren, Thomas E. Dewey, Edmund G. Brown, and Warren G. Magnuson. All came into prominence as fighting prosecutors, often basing their campaigns for higher political office on a reputation gained from a widely publicized investigation or trial.

The use of the office of prosecuting attorney as a stepping-stone to more prestigious governmental positions has long been recognized. Raymond Moley surveyed the lawyer-members of Congress from 1914 to 1926, and the governors of the states in 1920 and 1924, finding that 42 percent had been prosecuting attorneys early in their careers.[3] More recently Matthews found that half the members of the United States Senate began their careers in law enforcement either as prosecutors or judges.[4] Likewise, Schlesinger discovered that, although there was variation among the states, 32 percent of the governors had had careers in law enforcement.[5] A check of the *Congressional Directory* reveals that sixteen senators and sixty-one representatives in the 89th Congress list experience in the prosecutor's office.

This emphasis on the partisan political advantages accruing to the prosecuting attorney overshadows the political importance of his daily decisions. These exert a tremendous influence on the allocation of values in the community. Through the use of his discretionary powers the prosecutor is able to decide which cases will be prosecuted, the charges to be made, and the bargains to be agreed upon with the defendant. Like a judge or legislator, he has the power of and responsibility for making public policy. The policy made will reflect certain value priorities.

The prosecuting attorney using his discretionary powers influences the ways laws are enforced. This, in turn, shapes the behavior of citizens. A decision to "crack down" on vice through the harassment of prostitutes, homosexuals, or petty gamblers may be compared with the decision to ignore a case of assault by a respected member of the community at the local country club. In such cases the differences in the allocation of justice are obvious. The treatment accorded these groups raises numerous questions concerning the decision-making ability of the prosecutor, the role of community influentials, and the values of the community. The prosecutor has the authority to determine the cases that will be prosecuted, the type of charge that will be brought into the courtroom, and the level of enthusiasm with which he pursues a case, developing new evidence until a conviction is finally obtained. These decisions may be made on grounds other than evidential, and cannot be reviewed except by the electorate.

Of the many positions within the judicial process, the prosecutor's is distinctive in that it is concerned with all aspects of the system. Thus, the operations of the coroner's office, the grand jury, regulatory boards, and welfare agencies are directly affected by the ways in which the prosecutor carries out his responsibilities. Freund, who makes a distinction between enforcement and prosecutive powers, also points out that the prosecuting attorney is sharply differentiated from other administrative officers because of his close affiliation with the courts.[6] Accordingly, if we were to place the prosecutor's activities on a scale, we would see that at one end he performs many tasks concurrently and in cooperation with the police. He may, for instance, investigate areas of suspected wrongdoing, directing the police in the actual apprehension of law violators. At the other end of the scale, we would recognize him as an officer of the court, concerned in his role of adjudicator that justice be accorded defendants. In the United States where public prosecution is the exclusive means by which defendants are brought to trial, the prosecuting attorney is the vital link between the police and the courts.

References to "prosecutor's dilemma" are often found in legal literature. This dilemma arises because as a "lawyer for the state" he is expected to do everything in his power to win his client's case, yet he is also a member of the legal profession and expected to engage in prosecution not to convict, but to see that justice is done. The conditions under which he works are thought to create a "prosecutor's bias," sometimes called "prosecution complex." One of the injunctions placed upon the prosecutor is that he represent all of the people of his jurisdiction, including the accused. Thus, from a theoretical standpoint he may often be placed in the unenviable position of having to disclose evidence which may result in the destruction of his case. Yet, as a former deputy noted:

"A prosecutor is supposed to get to the truth, but I don't care what they say, he is an advocate. He believes in his case and his witnesses, and he wants to win. You really take a lot of razzing in the office if you don't. You might get a reputation for not trying to win."

The "prosecutor's dilemma" arises, then, because of a conflict between ethical injunctions and the values inherent in the environment of the organization within which he works.

As the nexus of the adjudicative and enforcement functions, the prosecutor has been called the most powerful single individual in local government. If he does not act, the judge and the jury are helpless and the policeman's word is meaningless. In this position, the prosecutor plays many roles, including crusader, administrator, counselor (to other government officials), and advocate. Each man occupying the position may interpret the roles according to the other(s) in the relationship, the environment within which he operates, and his own personality. The power of the prosecuting attorney was well stated by the Wickersham Commission in 1931:

"The prosecutor [is] the real arbiter of what laws shall be enforced and against whom, while the attention of the public is drawn rather to the small percentage of offenders who go through the courts."[7]

By following a criminal case through the judicial process we may readily understand the role of the prosecuting attorney in all phases of the allocation of justice. The type of case that reaches the courtroom and its disposition depend to a large extent upon the character of the local political structure. If we momentarily lay aside the influence of the prosecutor on the police, we can see that from the time that a suspect's case is turned over to the prosecutor, there are major decisions over which he has almost undisputed sway. Because of the prosecutor's discretionary powers he is able to make decisions that often allow him to become a key figure in the local political system.

After he has decided that a crime has been committed that

should be prosecuted, the prosecutor has great freedom to determine the type of charges. If, for instance, it is thought that the defendant entered a house at night carrying a weapon, stole a valuable piece of jewelry, and in the process assaulted the owner, there are many charges that it is possible for the prosecutor to enter. The type of charge may be influenced by such political considerations as the attitude of the press, the status of the defendant in the community, and the nearness of election day.

After the charge has been made, the prosecutor may decide if he will reduce the charge in exchange for a guilty plea or *nol. pros.*, thus ending the litigation. His decision may be dictated by his desire to create a good conviction record or because of a congested court calendar. Prosecuting attorneys are especially eager to impress the public with their record of convictions. They generally compute this by adding the number of guilty pleas to the number of trial convictions and dividing by the total number of cases processed. It is little wonder that most are able to boast a 98 percent conviction record when they run for re-election.

Upon the successful conclusion of a case, the prosecutor is able to exert influence over the sentence given by the judge. The prosecutor usually submits a recommendation to the judge concerning the nature of the sentence to be imposed. If he fails to convict the defendant, he may assemble additional evidence, change the charge, and pursue the case again.

The prosecuting attorney is required to play many roles in the allocation of justice. It is difficult to characterize him as involved primarily in law enforcement, administration, or adjudication. He takes an active part in all facets of the judicial process, and is, in a sense, the warp that binds the weft of the system. His capacity to make vital decisions without reference to specific injunctions is a major factor in the allocation of justice and serves to illuminate the politics of the process.

STRUCTURE OF THE OFFICE

The office of prosecutor is the epitome of decentralization. In most states he is responsible only to the voters and enjoys an independence from the formal checks usually placed upon public officials in American government. Although he is usually elected for a four-year term, there are few other public checks on his actions. As Mayers correctly indicates, the prosecuting attorney is either responsible to no one other than the voters or to the governor only for aggravated nonfeasance or misfeasance.[8] In most states neither the governor nor the attorney general is authorized to investigate suspected illegal activity without permission of the local prosecutor.

Not only is there a lack of structural elements which tie the prosecutor's decision-making power to those of other officials in the judicial process, but the confidential nature of his decisions lessens the visibility with which others may view his actions. For instance, a decision may result from a verbal agreement between a deputy prosecutor and a defense attorney conducted over a cup of coffee or in the hall outside the courtroom. Such an agreement may result in the reduction of a charge in exchange for a plea of guilty, or the dropping of the charge upon the willingness of the defendant to seek psychiatric help. If we stipulate that a decision maker's power increases as the opportunity for external anticipation, observation, and review decreases, then we may infer that the prosecutor's office is a major source of political power.

Relations with the Attorney General

One of the paradoxical conditions existing in the legal system is that most state governments have abdicated their function in criminal law enforcement. As Ploscowe states:

> "The laws which are enforced by police, prosecutor, and court are state laws, but their enforcement is left to the myriad of independent local law enforcement agencies, without adequate power anywhere to insist upon the decent standards of enforcement and cooperation or the adoption of uniform law enforcement policies."[9]

In almost all states the governor, the attorney general, and other state officials have no effective formal control over how the local prosecutor enforces statutes passed by the state legislatures.

Only the Pennsylvania Supreme Court has upheld the right of the attorney general to supersede the local prosecutor.[10] In most states the attorney general's power is limited to administrative controls such as requiring the prosecutor to submit reports on his activities. It is with civil cases that the attorney general is pretty much supreme.

Legal scholars have been concerned about this situation, especially in connection with prosecutors who have been either negligent or corrupt in the performance of their duties. In Washington and several states, control of the local law enforcement processes by the attorney general is dependent upon a call for assistance by the prosecutor or upon the request of the governor. The Washington constitution also provides for the removal of a prosecutor upon a joint resolution approved by three-fourths of the members of the legislature. Thus, only under extraordinary circumstances would the attorney general feel impelled to supersede the local prosecutor. Washington's attorney general, John O'Connell, reported that during his nine-year tenure in office he has never used the powers to supersede a county prosecutor. He has conducted informal investigations into conditions when it was apparent that the prosecutor was unable or unwilling to take action. The results have then been forwarded to the judges of the county involved for their consideration and action.

In 1959, O'Connell was asked by the judges of the Superior Court of Snohomish County to investigate a situation where it appeared that Prosecuting Attorney Arnold Zempel had knowingly allowed a house of prostitution to remain open. Zempel has been described as a "don't rock the boat politician" who possesses the flamboyance characteristic of the state's political past. This situation came to light in August, when Zempel's chief criminal deputy prosecutor, Lloyd Meeds, led a raid on the vice establishment without the prosecutor's knowledge. Two deputy sheriffs were found on the premises at the time of the raid, which eventually resulted in the indictment of Sheriff Robert Twitchell for willful neglect of duty and federal Mann

Act charges. At the same time charges were made implicating the county commissioners in illegal financial transactions concerning the sale of publicly owned property and the collection of political contributions.

In Washington a grand jury may be called only by the prosecuting attorney or a majority of the judges of the superior court. The conduct of the jury's proceedings is then the responsibility of the prosecutor. O'Connell investigated the charges surrounding his fellow Democrats in Snohomish County and reported his findings to the court. The judges called a grand jury but sought to by-pass the implicated prosecutor, asking the governor to direct O'Connell to appoint a special prosecutor. The judges later acknowledged that they were powerless to remove Zempel from the direction of the grand jury's investigation of his conduct. The impasse was resolved when pressure was successfully brought upon Zempel to appoint two special prosecutors, one from outside the county, to direct the grand jury. In characteristic humor, Zempel suggested that the judges might want to stand aside.

This case illustrates the prosecuting attorney's independence from formal checks on his power by other officials. Zempel was able to resist the formal demands of the attorney general and the county's top judicial body that he withdraw. He contended that to do so would be an admission of guilt. The only possible way in which the prosecutor's action could be formally checked would have been for the governor to declare that the legal system in the county had broken down.

Relations with County Government

Although the prosecuting attorney's responsibilities appear to be related primarily to criminal proceedings, he is also the legal counsel for county government in civil matters. He prosecutes violations of regulatory statutes, collects delinquent taxes, and represents the county against the claims of persons upon government. His opinions serve to guide public agencies in fulfilling their statutory goals.

The independence of the prosecutor from formal checks on

his authority is also a characteristic of his relationship with the county commissioners. In Washington, although he may not bring an action in the name of the county against the commissioners, they, in turn, are dependent upon him as counsel. This client relationship is much more complicated than the formal arrangements may indicate because the prosecutor depends upon the commissioners for his operating budget, while they must rely upon the prosecutor to enforce statutes which they pass. The fact that both offices are greatly involved in party politics adds a further dimension to the relationship.

Two days prior to the 1964 Seattle municipal elections, the Democratic majority among the King County commissioners passed a measure designed to prevent racial discrimination in the sale of real estate in unincorporated areas of the county. Although the effectiveness of this bill may be debated, the fact that the law passed so close to an election which included a referendum on a similar measure for Seattle has political significance. Since the Republican candidates for office opposed the measure, the political importance of the commissioners' action was increased.

Prosecutor Carroll announced that he would not enforce the new county statute because it had been passed illegally. He based his opinion on the fact that during the final hearing several changes had been made in it and that these materially changed its scope and effectiveness, thus making necessary another public hearing. According to County Commissioner Munro, Carroll's announcement came at the insistence of a number of Republican committeemen—"We make these changes all of the time, there was nothing wrong with the procedure."

Discretionary Powers of the Prosecutor

Rarely is the scope of the prosecutor's discretionary power either publicly recognized or defined by statute. Generally, state laws are explicit in requiring the prosecution of offenders, yet "nowhere in the laws is there to be found a specific enumeration of the elements" which must be present for the prosecutor to take action.[11] Most states describe the prosecutor's responsibility in such vague terms as "prosecuting all crimes and civil actions in which state or county may be party." On those occasions when the prosecutor's decisions have been challenged, they have been shielded from judicial inquiry by the invocation of the almost magical formula, "within the prosecutor's discretion." In essence, the American people have placed the district attorney in a position where he has to make choices, but they have not given him principles of selection.

When the prosecutor feels that the community no longer considers an act to constitute criminal behavior as prescribed by the law, he will probably refuse to prosecute or will expend every effort to convince the complainant that prosecution should be avoided. In this way he acts as the father confessor of the community. But, like other government officials, the prosecutor is sensitive to the force of public opinion. Often he must take measures to protect himself when he considers that a course of action is liable to arouse antipathy toward law enforcement rather than the accused. If he holds an exaggerated notion of duty he can arouse a storm of protest which may gain him the reputation of being a "persecutor," consequently losing the cooperation of the public and other agencies of the judicial system. As Lippmann has observed, "Without backing of public opinion, law enforcement officers are powerless."[12] It is therefore easy to understand why statutes prohibiting fornication or petty gambling are seldom invoked, even when their repeal cannot be expected. A New York prosecutor has remarked, "We are pledged to the enforcement [of the law]. but we have to use our heads in the process."

ORGANIZATION OF THE OFFICE

Located at the edge of Seattle's central business district in close proximity to the skid row area of Pioneer Square stands the bleak granite King County Courthouse. Like similar structures found in county seats throughout the United States, this imposing building houses all public officials responsible for the allocation of justice. Within the courthouse it is possible for a person to be held by the sheriff, to have criminal charges entered against him by the prosecutor, to be found guilty by a judge and jury, and finally to serve a portion of his term in the jail on the top floor. To the accused it must appear that the machinery of justice is primarily dependent upon the elevator that whisks him from one office to another—from the sheriff's on the tenth floor to the prosecutor's on the sixth, up to the eighth for trial and sentencing, and then the long ride to the twelfth for confinement in a cell.

Charles O. "Chuck" Carroll was appointed prosecuting attorney of King County in 1948 following the elevation of Prosecutor Lloyd Shorette to the Superior Court.[13] During his long tenure, Carroll has gained a reputation for running a clean office, but also an office that is not as aggressive as it might be. As a former Seattle mayor commented, "Carroll does all right when it comes down to the wire, but getting him there is another story."

An organization chart hanging in Carroll's office reflects the fact that the Office of King County Prosecuting Attorney is structured along functional lines, with divisions for criminal, civil, and domestic relations cases. The thirty-five deputy prosecutors are assigned to the divisions in numbers reflecting the case load and importance of the unit; twenty-two deputies man the Criminal Department, five are assigned to civil cases, while four deputies make up the Domestic Relations Department. Each is led by a chief deputy who reports directly to Carroll.

One other section, the Investigation Department, completes the formal organization. The duties assigned to this section reflect one of the inconsistent features of the system. The question has arisen as to whether the prosecutor should be engaged in the investigation of suspected illegal activity. Although the laws of many states require the prosecutor to investigate certain types of activities, Carroll publicly insists that he does not have investigative powers. For instance, he told the author "that [investigation] is the job for the sheriff and police. It's their job to bring me the charges." His predecessor, Lloyd Shorette, has an opposite conception:

"The prosecutor has the power of investigation and should use it. I raided the China Pheasant and closed it down two weeks after I took office, something Warner [Shorette's predecessor] didn't seem to get around to do. The prosecutor has the positive duty to step in when law enforcement breaks down. He is not supposed to be popular. He should stand at arm's length from the police, sheriff; he can't be buddy-buddy. He has an obligation to the public to force the hand of the law enforcement officer."

Carroll's annual report to the governor lists the duties of the four-man Investigation Department as the preparation of pre-sentence reports for the court. Most deputy prosecutors interviewed said that the prosecutor does use his investigators to check on the effectiveness of the police and to handle those "sensitive" cases involving political figures. In 1961, for instance, Carroll's investigation of suspected illegal actions by Commissioner Howard Odell resulted in Odell's speedy resignation. Since Carroll views his job as "keeping the lid on crime in King County," it would seem necessary that he have access to information concerning the underworld.

The reluctance of the prosecutor to acknowledge his investigative powers serves two purposes. First, it helps to maintain cordial relations with other law enforcement officials, specifically the police, in that he does not appear to be openly questioning their effectiveness. Second, by refusing to acknowledge his investigative powers the prosecutor is able to disclaim either the knowledge or ability to deal with those cases which indicate a laxity on the part of law enforcement agencies.

The functions of the Domestic Relations Department also need explanation. This office has two responsibilities: to prosecute non-support cases and to provide representation for the state in all divorce actions when only one party appears in court. The department's work is closely linked to the county welfare agency's Aid to Dependent Children program. State law requires that the prosecutor investigate all cases where these funds are allocated and determine if prosecution is suitable as a means of securing support for the children. To qualify for assistance, applicants are referred to the prosecutor so that non-support charges may be filed against the negligent mate.

In the eyes of most people, the Criminal Department is "where the action is." Staffed by a chief criminal deputy and his two assistants, plus a complement of twenty-two deputy prosecutors, it is the focal point of the system. Here decisions are made concerning charges, bargains with defense attorneys are negotiated, and cases prepared for trial.

Prior to Carroll's administration, the decision-making process in the Criminal Department was decentralized. Deputies were given the authority to make crucial decisions without coordinating their activities with other staff members. It was also possible for the police to choose the deputy they wished to handle a case. Under these conditions the habit of "shopping around" developed. The arresting officer would search the office to find a deputy who, on the basis of past experience, he knew would be sympathetic to the officer's attitude. A former deputy described this system as one in which there were no departmental policies concerning the treatment to be accorded various types of cases. As he noted, "It pretty much depended upon the police and their luck in finding the deputy they wanted."

Case assignment is now centralized under the direction of the chief criminal deputy. Prosecutors are expected to be able to handle all types of cases; however, several deputies have developed specialties based on their success in court. A female deputy is always assigned morals cases; because successful prosecution of such cases is dependent upon the victim's (usually a child or woman) testimony, it is felt that she will be better able to elicit the necessary information.

Compared with the activity in the Criminal Department, the Civil Department appears serene. As previously noted, the prosecuting attorney is concerned not only with violations of the criminal law, but also acts as counsel to county government in actions related to civil law. In this the Civil Department represents the interest of government in tax, garnishment, and zoning litigations. The various transactions concerning the financing of government, such as the issuance of bonds, must also come before the prosecutor's civil section.

STAFFING THE OFFICE—THE DEPUTIES

The training, competence, and goals of the members of an organization greatly affect the ways in which the processes of the institution are structured, for, as Herbert Simon has noted, "The problem of organization becomes inextricably interwoven with the problem of recruitment."[14] In an office composed of employees planning to devote their entire careers to the organization, we would expect that the institution's goals would be achieved in a manner different from one in which there was a constant change in personnel. In a fundamental way, then, the attitudes of the deputy prosecutors toward their futures in public service and the conditions under which they join the office will affect the expenditures of resources for their recruitment and training. Further, the rate by which the prosecutor's office is infused with "new blood" will greatly affect the degree of openness of the system, a basic element in the decisional process.

In a letter to a young lawyer, G. Clinton Fogwell advised that work in the prosecutor's office is fine if one is bent upon a political career, but "if you want a private practice, don't stay too long."[15] This view typifies remarks made by former deputy prosecutors interviewed by the author. Work as a deputy is seen as an excellent training, especially if a lawyer is planning a career which includes trial work. Not only is the experience in the office useful, but more important is the opportunity to obtain courtroom exposure. As one former deputy related, "In three years I tried three dozen jury cases. In a lifetime of private practice you would never get that many." Other respondents contended that you "get your 'court legs' faster" and have a chance to "get to know the bench and bar."

Although those with experience in the prosecutor's office believed that their time was well spent, they also thought that professionally it was dangerous to stay too long. A member of one of Seattle's larger law firms rejected the idea that the prosecutor's office is a good training ground:

"The prosecutor's office leads nowhere. If you go, try and get on the civil side because that is where you will get the most experience that

will benefit you later. We want lawyers what can aid business, not
those primarily experienced in criminal law."

When we note the orientation of the American bar with its
emphasis on the lawyer as advisor to corporations, we may
question the value of the benefits accruing to the young lawyer
from his prosecutorial experience; criminal matters are not
important in such practices.

The difficulty of moving from the criminal law orientation of
the prosecutor's office to the civil practice of the large law firm
was mentioned by several older members of the Seattle legal
community. It was pointed out that the skills developed in
criminal practice are not those required by the firm with a
corporate orientation. Rather, it was indicated that work in the
prosecutor's office can often mean that the young lawyer will
have lost ground with his law school contemporaries who have
come directly to the firm.

Other than the experience to be gained, the King County
Prosecutor's Office offers a financial inducement to the young
lawyer. In most instances a recent law school graduate can
expect to receive low compensation for the menial tasks which
he performs in an established firm. In the prosecutor's office,
however, he receives an initial salary that is higher than that he
would get from a private firm. Although this differential has
decreased in recent years, the prosecutor is still able to offer his
appointees at least $100 a month more than the average law
firm can offer. The prosecutor loses this advantage as the
deputy gains experience. After three years as a prosecuting
attorney the young lawyer is able to command a much higher
salary in the private sector.

Opportunities for promotion within the prosecutor's office
are slight, and hence act as an additional deterrent to the
assistant prosecutor with career objectives. Since the organization requires only a few supervisors and a large body of trial
lawyers, promotions to the top positions are few. Observation
of the King County Prosecutor's Office revealed that the tasks
performed and responsibilities given to both the newest and
senior assistant were essentially the same, the only exception
being that the more senior prosecutors were usually given the
more difficult cases.

Fogwell's advice, together with the financial and promotion circumstances, combine to cause a high turnover rate among deputy prosecutors in King County. As one deputy related, "When you go to work for Carroll there is an understanding that you will stay at least three years. When that time is up, it's time to go!" An examination of the tenure of deputies interviewed reveals that the average length was three years and four months. The financial attractions of private practice, plus the expectation that one will escape the "red tape of bureaucracy," induce most deputies to leave the prosecutor's office.

The turnover among deputies is one of the major problems facing the prosecutor. This is disruptive in a bureaucracy where reputations and informal understandings are key elements in the decision-making process. In addition, new prosecutors require the allocation of resources for training purposes. The frustrations of having to recruit and train deputies on a continuing basis were noted by Carroll:

> "It takes at least six months before I can send a new man to court on his own and two years to train someone who is able to handle a tough case in Superior Court. Some don't get that far. As soon as we have a good man who can make a record for himself he is snatched up by the big firms."

Appointment to the prosecutor's staff in King County generally involves partisan political considerations:

> "Carroll believes that the office is a political one, and this is made clear to you when you accept an appointment. The staff is expected to be involved in his campaigns and not to work for anyone else."

With some exceptions, candidates must be of the same party as the prosecutor and secure letters of recommendation from some of the "big dome Republicans." On those occasions when Carroll has appointed Democrats, he has insisted that they discontinue active participation in their party for the duration of their appointment. It is important, however, to have at least one deputy on the staff who is publicly known as a member of the opposite political party. Such a man is useful to the prosecutor when he is confronted with a case involving a high Democratic official, especially if there are political ramifications to the situation. To avoid the charge that prosecution has been initiated out of political considerations, a deputy with the same party affiliation as that of the defendant is assigned the case.

The weakness of party organizations in Washington is shown by the fact that Carroll has been able to resist the criticisms of party leaders when he has appointed members of the opposition:

> "The Republican County Chairman accused me of being a Democrat and wanted Carroll to fire me. Carroll is vindictive, and independent enough, so that he told the chairman that he would hire whom he wanted to hire."

However, when he has needed the cooperation of the party, as in 1956 when he considered a race for the governorship, Carroll has been careful to clear appointments with the leadership.

Although ethnic politics is not usually considered a dominant characteristic of King County, especially when comparisons are made to the urban centers of the East Coast, this variable is important in securing appointment to the prosecutor's office. Carroll takes pains to be sure that "there are representatives of the various 'communities' " among his deputies. In a style characteristic of the politics of New York and Chicago, a number of positions are tagged as "belonging" to certain ethnic and religious groups, and are regularly allotted to deputies with Jewish, Negro, and Oriental backgrounds. As one attorney related:

> "I was known as an active Democrat doing work for the NAACP and ADL when Carroll sought me out. He was looking for his "Jewish Deputy" since Murray Guterson was just leaving."

Other "hyphenated Americans" representing the Greek, Italian, and Scandinavian communities are included among Carroll's staff, but with more apparent flexibility in their appointments than deputies from the previously mentioned groups.

On the basis of interviews with the deputies and analysis of personnel records, a composite may be drawn of the typical assistant prosecutor in the King County office during 1964: a recent graduate of the University of Washington Law School who joined the office within two years of passing the bar examination, who became a prosecutor when he was twenty-seven years old, and who plans to remain for the agreed-upon three years. So high is the tendency for assistant prosecutors to possess these characteristics that only four deviate to any extent from the composite. These four joined Carroll's office for a variety of reasons late in their careers. One, for instance, became a deputy when a heart condition necessitated that he eschew private practice for the "lighter" work of the prosecutor's office. A second deputy, a woman who was graduated from law school when she was fifty years old, joined the staff because both her sex and age were considered obstacles to a successful private practice. The other deviants were judged by their colleagues to be "poor lawyers who couldn't make it on the outside." These four will be discussed below as investigation reveals that they may be also considered the "locals" in the prosecuting attorney's office.

With thirty-five lawyers authorized for his staff, the prosecutor could use his office as a training ground for aspiring candidates for his party's nomination to public office. The opportunities are available for a deputy to achieve public notice through his being assigned to newsworthy cases, and by representing the prosecutor at official functions. As one candidate for prosecutor related, "If I had been elected I would have used the office to train and launch aspiring Democrats. This would be a real source of political power for myself and the party." Although several deputies have run for the state legislature, Carroll has not utilized the position for political purposes of this nature. Many observers stated that they thought that Carroll does not want to take the chance of a challenge from one of his deputies.

There is a tendency for deputies to form partnerships with other former prosecutors when they begin private practice. Of the eighteen deputies who joined the King County staff in 1959, ten are now associated with other former deputies. In fact, one firm consists of four partners, all of whom worked together in the prosecutor's office. Several of the respondents noted that the friendships formed during their tenure as prosecutors helped immeasurably when they started to practice in the private sector. Because they were familiar with the policies and procedures of Carroll's office, they were able to advance their clients' causes in ways not available to most lawyers.

The deputy prosecuting attorney may be viewed as a professional who works in a bureaucracy. He has been socialized through his legal training and contacts with fellow attorneys to the ethics of the law community, yet he has accepted employment in an organization with somewhat different goals and expectations. Although the bar has long been typified by the independent practitioner, there has been a recent increase in the number of attorneys who are "salarists"—professionally trained persons employed by public agencies. For example, the American Bar Foundation reported that 20 percent of the attorneys in the United States were wholly engaged in work for public organizations.[16] The percentage of professionals in bureaucracy is increasing at a dramatic rate.

As "old" professions such as the law look to large-scale organizations as the focus of their work, conflicts can be seen. Because the lawyer-bureaucrat becomes less directly dependent on the professional community for his career advancement, the ordinary sanctions of that community may have less impact. There may also be conflicts within the bureaucracy between the professionally oriented person and the specific, particularist task requirements of his organization. Merton, Gouldner, and others have noted the differences in orientation between those "cosmopolitan" persons who maintain a professional outlook and those "locals" whose basic loyalty is to the bureaucracy.[17] The "cosmopolitan" seeks satisfaction and recognition outside the organization's environs, while the "local" has often cut his professional ties and seeks satisfaction through the narrow confines of his organization.

The concepts of cosmopolitan and local can be applied to an urban prosecuting attorney's office. According to Gouldner's criteria, cosmopolitans could be expected to view their short tenure as an opportunity to gain experience before advancing to a position in a law firm, rather than the "career within bureaucracy" outlook of the local. The cosmopolitan maintains membership in professional groups such as the bar association, while the local pursues his interest in organizations with other public employees. The career of the local rises and falls with that of the organization, hence, he is interested in promoting the goals of the agency and improving its status within the bureaucratic structure.

Interviews with the deputy prosecutors in King County revealed that although the predominant number were cosmopolitan, four could be classified as local. It is of particular interest to note that the local deputies did not handle criminal cases, but were assigned to the Civil and Domestic Relations Departments, areas where there is greater reliance upon knowledge of administrative procedures and less upon discretion. It could also be suggested that since the cosmopolitan is less bound by organizational pressures, he would tend to greater interest in the clients of the prosecutor's office, especially if such conduct were appropriate in professional terms. The separation of the locals from the cosmopolitans within the formal office structure probably served to reduce potential conflicts between the types. The career patterns of the locals were also different from the cosmopolitans. Those whose loyalty was to the bureaucracy were older and had engaged in private practice before assuming a position with the prosecutor. One local said that he left private practice because of ill health and desire to work at a slower pace. The locals, unlike the cosmopolitans, expressed a loyalty to their organization and were willing to continue to work in the bureaucracy.

EXCHANGE RELATIONS

As we have continuously stressed, the formal rules do not completely account for the behavior of the organization's actors, since an informal structure also exists which results from the social environment and the interaction of these actors. As the focal organization in an exchange system, it has been assumed that the office of prosecuting attorney makes decisions which reflect the influence of its clientele. In this system there are different levels of interaction between the prosecutor and his various clients. Some, such as criminal lawyers, are constantly in contact with the office, while others, such as the general public may only periodically activate its role in the exchange system.

Figure II-1 outlined some of the exchange relationships existing between the office of prosecuting attorney and its clientele. In this section the nature of selected exchange relationships will be discussed, using the evidence from the Seattle study. No attempt has been made either to estimate the extent of these interactions or to indicate some of the potential clients of the office. As previously noted, the office will be tied to its clients through the actions of personnel playing various roles. Some clients have access to only one role player, while others may tie themselves to the prosecutor through a complex of exchange relationships involving a number of actors in the decisional process. Since this book is organized to follow the progression of decision-making within the criminal justice system, such important activities as plea bargaining will be discussed in a later portion.

At this point it is important to call attention to Grosman's idea that the "winner take all" solution to legal problems and the adversary theory of conflict is undermined when there is a possibility of common gain through cooperation between partners in an exchange relationship. In this case, the concept of the prosecutor as a quasi-judicial officer of the court lends credence to non-adversarial activity of bargaining.

Police

Although the prosecuting attorney has discretionary power to determine the disposition of cases, he is dependent upon the police as the only source of the raw materials with which he works. Because of the low visibility of police decisions and his own lack of investigative resources, the prosecutor is unable to exercise the desired affirmative control over the types of cases brought to him for disposition. Input materials include not only cases, but also the evidence from the police which will help to convict the offender. No prosecutor wants to have poorly developed cases dumped in his lap.

In his relationships with the police, the prosecutor is not without countervailing powers. His main check is his ability to return cases for further investigation and to refuse to approve arrest warrants. The police depend upon the prosecutor to accept the output of their system; rejection of too many cases can have serious repercussions affecting the morale and discipline of the force.

A request for prosecution may be turned down for a number of reasons unrelated to the facts of the case. First, the prosecutor serves as a regulator of caseloads not only for his own office, but for the rest of the judicial bureaucracy. Constitutional and statutory time limits prevent him and the courts from building a backlog of untried cases. A second reason for rejecting prosecution requests may stem from the prosecutor's thinking of his public exposure in the courtroom; he does not want to take forward cases which will place him in an embarrassing position. Finally the prosecutor may return cases to check the quality of police work. As a former chief criminal deputy said, "You have to keep them on their toes, otherwise they get lazy. If they aren't doing their job, leak the situation to the newspapers." Rather than spend the resources necessary to find additional evidence, the police may dispose of a case by sending it back to the prosecutor on a lesser charge, may implement the "copping-out machinery" leading to a guilty plea, may drop the case, or, in some instances they may send it to the corporation counsel for action in municipal court.

In most cases, a deputy prosecutor and the assigned police officer occupy boundary-spanning roles in this exchange relationship. Deputies reported that after repeated contacts they got to know the policemen whom they could trust. As one said, "There are some you can trust, others you have to watch because they are trying to get rid of cases on you." Deputies may be influenced by the officer's attitude on a case. One officer noted to a deputy in the presence of thy author that he had a weak case, but mumbled, "I didn't want to bring it up here, but that's what they wanted." As might be expected, the deputy turned down prosecution on the case.

Sometimes the police perform the ritual of "shopping

around," seeking a deputy prosecutor who, on the basis of past experience, is liable to be sympathetic to their view on a case. At one time this practice was so widespread that staff members were instructed to ascertain from the police officer if he had seen another deputy about a case. Even though the office now has a centralized systems for the allocation of cases, the author noted that it is possible for the police to request a specific deputy. Often a prosecutor has a reputation for specializing in a type of case; this may mean that the police assume that he will get the case anyway, so they skirt the formal procedure and bring it to him directly.

One source of friction between the prosecutor and the chief of police in Seattle is the chain of command within the judicial system. Former Mayor Gordon Clinton alleged that "Carroll thinks that because he is prosecutor, the Seattle Police Department is under his jurisdiction and not the mayor's." Respondents said that there have been several disputes among the prosecutor, mayor, and chief, especially in regard to the enforcement policy toward gambling. However, it must be noted that on several occasions, when there has been a public outcry, the police and prosecutor have closed ranks.

An exchange relationship between a deputy prosecutor and a police officer may be influenced by the type of crime at stake. The prototype of a criminal is a robber—one who violates person and property. However, a large number of cases have to do with "crimes without victims." This term refers to those crimes which are violations of moral codes, where the general public is theoretically the complainant. In violations of laws against bookmaking, prostitution, and narcotics, the other actor in the transaction is not interested in having an arrest made. Hence, vice control men must drum up their own business. Without a civilian complainant, victimless crimes give the police and prosecutor greater leeway in determining the charges to be filed.

One area of exchange between the prosecutor's office and the police is that of narcotics control. As Skolnick notes, "The major organizational requirement of narcotics policing is the presence of an informational system."[19] Without a network of informers it is impossible to capture addicts and peddlers with evidence that can bring about convictions. One source of informers is among those arrested for narcotics violations. Through promises to reduce charges or even to *nol. pros.*, arrangements can be made so that the accused will return to the narcotics "community" and gather information for the police. Bargaining observed between the head of the narcotics squad of the Seattle force and the deputy prosecutor who specialized in drug cases, involved the question of charges, promises, and the release of an arrested peddler.

In the course of post-arrest questioning by the police, a well-known drug dealer intimated that he could provide evidence against a pharmacist suspected of illegally selling narcotics. Not only did the police representative want to transfer the case to the "friendlier" hands of a certain deputy, but he wanted to arrange for a reduction of charges and bail. He believed that it was important that the accused be let out on bail in such a way that the narcotics community would not realize that he had become an informer. He also had to insure that the reduced charges would be processed so that the informer could be kept "on the string," thus maintaining control of the narcotics squad over him. The deputy prosecutor, on the other hand, insisted on procedures that would not discredit the office. He "suggested" that the squad "work a little harder" on another pending case.

Courts

Like other agencies in the system, the courts have had to devise adaptive measures to deal with the problem of mass production. Adaptation has meant that certain basic assumptions underlie the judicial process: efforts are made to induce guilty pleas as a way of reducing the number of trials, the prosecutor brings to the courtroom only cases which he believes will result in conviction, and minor offenses are handled in volume. As shown in Table IV-1, the system operates so that only a small number of cases arrives for trial, the rest being disposed of through reduced charges, *nol. pros.*, and guilty

TABLE IV-1

DISPOSITION OF FELONY CASES—KING COUNTY, 1964

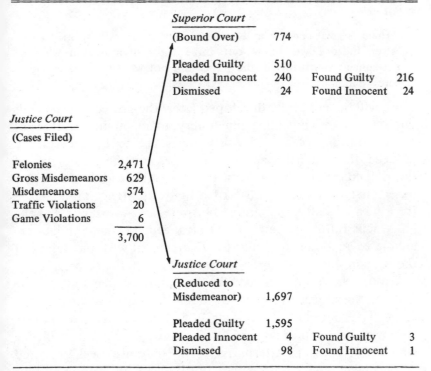

Superior Court			
(Bound Over)	774		
Pleaded Guilty	510		
Pleaded Innocent	240	Found Guilty	216
Dismissed	24	Found Innocent	24

Justice Court	
(Cases Filed)	
Felonies	2,471
Gross Misdemeanors	629
Misdemeanors	574
Traffic Violations	20
Game Violations	6
	3,700

Justice Court			
(Reduced to Misdemeanor)	1,697		
Pleaded Guilty	1,595		
Pleaded Innocent	4	Found Guilty	3
Dismissed	98	Found Innocent	1

SOURCE: Washington, Prosecuting Attorney of King County, *Annual Report*, 1964.

pleas. Not indicated are those cases removed by the police and prosecutor prior to the filing of charges.

The ways used by the court to dispose of cases is a vital influence in the judicial system. The court's actions effect pressures upon the prison system, the conviction rate of the prosecutor, and the work of probation agencies. The judge's decisions act as clues to other parts of the system, indicating the type of decision likely to be taken in future cases.

The influence of the courts on the decision to prosecute is very real. The sentencing history of each judge gives the prosecutor, as well as other enforcement officials, indication of the treatment a case may receive in the courtroom. The prosecutor's expectation as to the court's action may limit his discretion over the decision to prosecute. One deputy commented:

> "There is great concern as to whose court a case will be assigned. After Judge Lewis threw out three cases in a row in which entrapment was involved, the police did not want us to take any cases to him."

As will be more fully developed later, the prosecutor depends upon the plea bargaining machinery to maintain the flow of cases from his office. If guilty pleas are to be successfully induced, the sentencing actions of judges must be predictable. If the defendant and his lawyer are to be influenced to accept a lesser charge or the promise of a lighter sentence in exchange for a plea of guilty, there must be some basis to believe that the judge will fulfill his part of the arrangement. Since judges are unable to announce formally their agreement with the details of the bargain, their past performance influences the actors.

Within the limits imposed by law and the demands of the system, the prosecutor may regulate the flow of cases to the court. He may control the length of time between accusation and trial, hence he may hold cases until he has the evidence which will convict. Alternatively, he may also seek repeated adjournment and continuances until the public's interest dies down, witnesses may become unavailable, or other difficulties make his request for dismissal of prosecution more justifiable. Further, he may determine the type of court to receive the case and the judge who will hear it.

Many misdemeanors covered by state law are also violations of city ordinances. It is common practice for the prosecutor to send a misdemeanor case to the corporation counsel for processing in the municipal court when it is believed that a conviction may not be secured in justice court. As one former deputy said, "If there is no case—send it over to the city court. Things are speedier, less formal over there."

A person arrested on a felony charge must be given a preliminary hearing in a justice court within ten days. For the prosecutor, the preliminary hearing is an opportunity to evaluate the testimony of witnesses, to assess the strength of the evidence, and to try to predict the outcome of the case if it is sent to trial. Subsequently the prosecutor has several options: he may bind over the case for trial in Superior Court, he may reduce the charges to those of a misdemeanor for trial in justice court, or he may conclude that he has no case and drop the charges. Judge James Dore, President Judge of the Justice Courts of King County, estimates that about 70 percent of the felonies are reduced to misdemeanors after the preliminary hearing.

Besides having some leeway in determining the type of court in which to file a case, the prosecutor also has some flexibility in selecting the judge to receive the case. Until recently the prosecutor could file a case with a specific judge. "The trouble was that Judge——was erratic and independent, no one would file a case with him. The other judges objected that they were handling the entire workload, so a central filing system was devised." Under this procedure cases are assigned to the judges in rotation. However, as the chief criminal deputy commended, "The prosecutor can hold a case until the 'correct' judge comes up."

Community Influentials

As a part of the political system, the judicial process responds to the environment of the community. The exchange relationship between the community and the prosecutor's office may be analyzed at several levels. First, as the literature on the judicial process notes, the general public is able to have its values translated into policies followed by law enforcement officers. As Banfield tells us, the public cannot be disregarded by a formal organization as it seeks to maintain and enhance its own needs.[21] Through the political process, especially in the election of the prosecutor and the allocation of resources to his office, the electorate may influence decision-making.

The public's influence is particularly acute in those "gray areas" of the law where full enforcement is not expected. Legislatures may enact statutes which define the outer limits of criminal conduct, yet this does not necessarily mean that the laws will be fully enforced. Some statutes may be passed as expressions of desirable morality, while others are kept deliberately vague. Finally, there are some laws describing behavior which the community no longer considers criminal. A prosecutor's charging policies will reflect the public's attitude toward the legislation. He usually will not prosecute violations of laws regulating some forms of gambling, certain sexual practices, or "Sunday Blue Laws." For example, as a general practice prosecutors do not charge persons with "lewd and lascivious cohabitation" except when the complainant has seen the defendants in the act of sexual intercourse, a minor is involved, and the case arouses public attention.

Alternatively, the community may insist that prosecution be brought against those who upset its dominant values: groups with unorthodox political views may be harassed by the "red squad," civil rights workers may be prosecuted for a wide variety of violations, and "hippies" may be subjected to constant attempts by the police to discourage their activities. The public is also prone to insist that some forms of "immoral" activity be prosecuted, while persons in a higher social class engaged in the same pursuit are immune. Hence prostitutes in the poorer section of the community may be arrested, while their fellow professionals go unharmed as "hostesses" in the more expensive clubs and hotels.

Studies have shown the public's level of attention to public affairs is much lower than had been suspected:

> "So long as the vagrants are kept off the streets, the burglars away from the financial district, commercial vice and organized racketeering away from the middle class suburbs and the occasional spectacular case is somehow 'cracked' . . ."

the public is apathetic to the activities within the judicial process. Still, the community remains a potential source of pressure which may be activated by opinion leaders against the prosecutor.

Because the general public is a possible threat to the prosecutor, staff members take measures to protect him from criticism. Decision-making occurs with the public in mind—"will a course of action arouse antipathy towards the prosecutor rather than the accused?" Several deputies mentioned what they called the "aggravation level" of a crime. This is a recognition that the commission of certain crimes, within a specific context, will bring about a vocal reaction.

> "If a little girl walking home from the grocery store is pulled into the bushes and indecent liberties are taken, this is more disturbing to the public's conscience than a case where the father of the girl takes indecent liberties with her at home."

The Office of King County Prosecuting Attorney has a policy requiring that deputies file all cases involving sexual molestation in which the police believe the girl's story. The office also prefers charges in all negligent homicide cases where there is the least possibility of guilt. In these types of cases the public may respond to the emotional context of the case and demand prosecution. To "cover" the prosecutor from criticism, it is thought that the safest measure is to prosecute.

The public is also a source of new inputs to the prosecution system. Although most suspects are arrested by warrants initiated by the police, citizens may bring complaints to the attention of the prosecuting attorney, which can result in arrest. Because of this procedure the prosecutor is constantly bombarded with reports from citizens seeking action against persons assumed to have committed a crime. Such complaints, known as "generals" in the King County office, cover the spectrum from murder to ownership of barking dogs.

The deputy prosecutor receiving the "general" must determine if it is the concern of the prosecutor or if it should be referred to some other agency, such as the attorney general's Consumer Protection Division or the county welfare department. Respondents indicated that a very large portion of the complaints involved actions which should be handled by a lawyer in private practice.

It is also necessary to determine something about the motives of the complainant. Often the threat of prosecution is made to hasten the payment of debts. Prosecutor Carroll has insisted that he is not running a collection agency. Marital discord can also lead to attempts by one mate to file criminal charges against the other. Monday morning often finds a number of disturbed women in the prosecutor's office for this purpose; by doing so they hope to "pay back" their mates for misconduct. Although such charges may be properly filed, the prosecutor must determine the strength of a woman's commitment because often she will have second thoughts.

Another community group which engages in exchange relationships with the prosecutor is composed of those leaders who have a continuing or potential interest in the politics of prosecution. This group, analogous to the players in one of Long's community games, is linked to the prosecutor because his actions affect their success in playing another game. Hence community boosters may want either a crackdown or a hands-off policy toward gambling, political leaders may want the prosecutor to remember the interests of the party, and business leaders may want policies which will not interfere with their game. As Carroll said, "I am always getting pressures from different interests—business, the Chamber of Commerce, and labor. I have to try and maintain a balance between them." In exchange for these considerations the prosecutor may gain prestige, political support, and admission into the leadership groups.

Pressure by an interest group was evidenced during a strike by drugstore employees during December, 1964. The unions urged Carroll to invoke a state law which requires the presence of a licensed pharmacist if the drugstore is open. Not only did union representatives meet with Carroll, but picket lines were set up outside the courthouse protesting his refusal to act. The prosecutor resisted the pressure tactics.

Community leaders may also receive special treatment by the prosecutor if they run afoul of the law. A policy of the King County office is that cases involving prominent local persons be referred immediately to the chief criminal deputy and the prosecutor for disposition. One deputy remarked, "These cases can be pretty touchy. It's important that the boss knows immediately about this type of case so that he is not caught 'flat footed' when asked about it by the press."

Although prominent members of the community may

attempt to influence the prosecutor when their own interests are involved, there are times when the prosecutor's activities are a concern of community influentials. The evidence seems to indicate that in the case of Teamster President Dave Beck concerted action by a number of local leaders, who felt that the disclosures of the McClellan Committee were harmful to Seattle, overcame the prosecutor's objections and resulted in the calling of a grand jury.

A Grand Jury for Dave Beck

The story is told about the mayor of Seattle who said in 1936, "Dave Beck runs this town and I tell you it's a good thing he does."[22] At one time many Seattleites assumed that Beck did indeed run their town. Following his victory over the CIO in the organizing fights of the late 1930's, he cultivated close relations with the business community, turned the union to a conservative ideology, and gained respectability by his appointment to the University of Washington's Board of Regents. Although he did not take a direct part in local politics, he made a practice of contributing to the campaigns of incumbents and sure winners.

It must have been with some concern that Seattle's leaders read the McClellan Committee's disclosures about Beck in early 1957. Beck became the center of the committee's inquiry into illegal activities in the Teamsters union. From evidence gathered by Robert F. Kennedy, committee counsel, it appeared that Beck was guilty of misappropriation of union funds.[23] As the investigations continued, Kennedy criticized Seattle officials for not taking legal action under Washington laws, a criticism especially directed at Carroll, who had been long a friend and political ally of Beck.[24] As a former prosecuting attorney of the county noted, "It would have been awfully hard for Carroll to file charges against Dave Beck."

The city's leaders were particularly upset that the disclosures were attracting national attention and also that the statute of limitations deadline was nearing on many of the offenses said to have been committed by Beck. Pressure was mounted by various persons who urged that a grand jury be called to look into the charges.

Carroll responded by saying that he did not contemplate action because he did not have evidence that would hold up in court. Further, he asserted that there was not reason to call a grand jury since he had assigned his deputy, Charles Z. Smith, to act as a liaison with the committee to gather evidence. However, as George Martin, former president of the Washington State Bar Association, states, "If Carroll didn't have the information, there was all the more reason to call a grand jury, since it has subpoena powers and the prosecutor doesn't." Many politicians fear a grand jury because, once called, there are no limits to its investigative powers; it may expand its search into other areas and may become too powerful. As a result of mounting pressure, an attempt was made to get the King County Superior Court to call a grand jury. The judges wanted a grand jury, but did not want to be the instigators of it. "One judge even suggested that what the court should do is tell the public that Carroll should prosecute."

On April 14, 1957, the Board of Governors of the Washington State Bar Association passed a resolution requesting the judges of the Superior Court to call a grand jury to study the charges against Beck, specifically an investigation of the misuse of union funds, of the distribution of political contributions, and of a conspiracy between union leaders and employers. Martin has said that various community leaders put pressure on the bar to instigate the proceedings. Influential members of the Seattle community felt that it was necessary to "clear the air" and preserve the city's reputation.

On April 26 the Superior Court ordered a grand jury called. As previously mentioned, the judges may force the calling of a grand jury; however, the prosecutor is charged with guiding its actions. The King County judges assembled a list of persons who were qualified to serve as counsel for the jury. Carroll did not follow their advice and appointed instead former Seattle mayor and fellow Republican, William F. Devin, as special prosecutor. Martin declared, "This was unfortunate since Devin had too many political connections, was not a trial lawyer, and hadn't been in a courtroom for years."

By the time that the grand jury was called, the statute of limitations meant that most of the charges against Beck could not be aired. Carroll did charge Beck with larceny resulting from the acquisition of an automobile from the union. Carroll claimed,

"There was no reason to call the grand jury. I had Smith looking over the evidence and there wasn't anything I could use. The Statute of Limitations had run out. It took a team of accountants poring over files to find by mistake that Beck had gotten a car from the Teamsters."

Beck was found guilty of larceny, and was indicted in federal district court for income tax evasion.

THE DECISION TO PROSECUTE

In a summary statement of its findings on prosecutorial decision-making, the American Bar Foundation notes that the proceedings

"to determine whether a prosecution should be brought and to determine the nature of the charge, is in general characterized by its informality and the freedom to participate on the part of any individual or agency having an interest in the outcome."[25]

As stressed by the exchange model, decision-making is a product of the needs and goals of the system, as influenced by the environment in which it exists. As noted above, the decision to prosecute is not made at only one point in the judicial process. It is true that a decision to file charges is made during the initial phase, but the charges may be altered at any time by the prosecutor.

It is difficult to determine the exact motivation of a decision maker when he selects one alternative over another. Actors in the process may list the facts which entered into a specific decision, but these must be considered only surface reasons. As Pool has indicated,

"When a policy maker reaches a decision, he knows what conscious factors enter into it. But he seldom knows what conversations that he has had or words that he has read were responsible for initially injecting those ideas into his head, or reinforcing them, or turning them into final convictions."[26]

The social scientist must remember this problem so that he will not neglect the complexities of decision-making as he attempts to describe the process.

Interviews with King County deputy prosecutors revealed that there is a remarkable consensus on the standards used in the decision to prosecute. This can be explained not only by the fact that there are departmental policy guides or that the deputies are taught the norms of prosecution by the same instructors, but rather that interaction among the deputies is a strong builder of consensus. In the office setting, deputies are constantly visiting each other and exchanging information about cases, the habits of judges, and the preferences of the prosecutor. New deputies are encouraged to ask for the assistance of the more experienced prosecutors when they take their initial cases.

At the same time that there is latitude for the exchange of information among deputies, there are also norms which operate to create a competitive atmosphere within the office. The belief is widely held that the quality of a deputy is in part related to his success in securing convictions. This is challenged by Prosecutor Carroll, who insists that there are a number of factors which are used when promotions are considered. Still, as one deputy held, "No one wants to lose a case. You don't want to get a reputation for not being able to 'cut the mustard.' " Because their own records are at stake, deputies appeared to be extremely cautious in prosecution decisions. When a deputy authorizes prosecution, there is the possibility that he may eventually be the one to take the case to the courtroom. Kaplan notes,

"The criticism, or more usually, unwelcome sympathy produced by the loss of a case was generally far in excess of the congratulations produced by winning one, the assistant did not wish to authorize his own prosecution of a dubious case or saddle one of his cohorts with the trial of a 'turkey.' "[27]

Respondents tended to place those factors which are influential in the decision to prosecute into three categories: (A) Evidential, (B) Humanitarian, and (C) Organizational. It is impossible to say that one of these considerations is more important than another to a decision maker. At the initial stage, however, when a decision to file is made, the type and amount of evidence reflected by the police report appear to be a dominant factor. A former chief criminal deputy said, "If you have the evidence you file, then bring the other considerations in during the bargaining phase."

A. Evidential. —"Is there a case?" "Does the evidence warrant the arrest of an individual and the expense of a trial?" These are two of the major questions asked by a prosecutor when he is deciding if he should prosecute. The county prosecutor must ascertain is a crime has been committed which is viewed as a violation of the criminal law within the context of the local political system. As mentioned above, there are many borderline offenses committed under marginal circumstances which will not result in prosecution. In King County, for example, the offenses of attempted suicide and fornication are not prosecuted.

The nature of the crime may require that evidence be presented which can prove such broadly defined terms as "neglect" or "intent." The prosecutor must be certain that the evidence will coincide with the court's interpretation of these terms. Often the facts of the case may be clear, but the ambiguity of the law makes application of the facts difficult.

One other evidential factor concerns the nature of the complaint. As one deputy related, "We must consider for whose benefit prosecution is being undertaken." Often when complaints are entered by the general public they concern marital squabbles, neighborhood quarrels, or quasi-civil offenses. The prosecutor must differentiate those cases viewed as crimes against society from those which have been instigated for the personal benefit of the complainant.

"We can't act as a collection agency. There was the case of the firm which had three partners, then one bought the other two out, but they remained on as employees. The two took money from bills paid by customers without authorization as payment for salaries. The owner tried to start a prosecution to get the others to pay up.

"Sometimes we get a case where a wife wants us to prosecute her husband for assault or something. Usually she just wants to scare him, and drops the complaint when he comes home."

The role of prosecutor demands that factors of evidence be considered before a decision to file is made. Evidence is considered weak when it is difficult to use in proving charges, when the value of a stolen article is questionable, when a case results from a brawl, or when there is lack of corroboration.

B. *Humanitarian.*—The prosecutor is able to individualize justice in ways which can benefit both the accused and society. Especially when the offense stems from conduct arising from mental illness, the prosecutor may feel that some form of psychiatric treatment is required rather than imprisonment. "If the difficulty is of a mental character and the accused is eager for psychiatric help, prosecution may be deferred to afford him the opportunity." Before prosecutors drop criminal charges on the promise that medical help will be sought, they must have some guarantee that the care will be secured. If the accused is unable to afford the treatment, charges may be filed with the expectation that the judge will commit the accused to a state medical facility.

Protection of the victim may also be a reason for deciding against prosecution. In cases involving the sexual molestation of a child, prosecution may not be sought if conviction hinges on the testimony of the victim. If there is a possibility that psychological damage to the child might result from the courtroom experience, actions other than prosecution may be taken.

The character of the accused, his status in the community, and the impact of prosecution on his family may be factors influencing the charge files. The American Bar Foundation found that in some jurisdictions prosecution is not sought against middle-aged women accused of shoplifting. Prosecutors believe, and research suggests, that during the menopausal period there are definite tendencies toward kleptomania. Such considerations as the foregoing were viewed as humanitarian accommodations by respondents. One former prosecutor remarked:

> "We have to think about all of the facts in a case. Is the accused a first offender? Will a felony charge ruin his career? Should the charge be rape or sexual psychopath? Murder or manslaughter? The prosecutor has to make some important decisions for which there are no standards."

In 1964 a prominent lawyer was accused of stabbing a fellow attorney during an argument in the Seattle Yacht Club. Charges were not filed by either the police or the victim until after the newspapers described the incident. The inaction aroused suspicions that the prosecutor's office had succumbed to pressure from elites in the community to suppress the case. Finally the assailant was charged with a misdemeanor even though the facts suggested that a felony had been committed. Because the lawyer would be disbarred if convicted of a felony, it was explained that he had been accused of the lesser charge for humanitarian reasons. In this case the status of the accused, the location of the incident, and the consequences for his career affected the type of charge filed.

C. Organization. —The exchange relationships among units of the judicial system, the political environment of the community, and the resource demands placed upon the system influence the decision to prosecute. Although many of these factors have previously been examined, there are other organizational stresses which may preclude prosecution.

Certainly the question "What will be the reaction of the public?" looms over every decision. There is, of course, always a hard core of criminal cases that cannot be compromised. The heinous nature of the crime, the pressure of publicity, and the influence of complaining victims circumscribe the prosecutor's discretion. He might be less inclined to press charges of carnal knowledge involving an eighteen-year-old male and seventeen-year-old female than he would be if the case involved an older man and a younger girl. From a political standpoint a prosecutor feels that he must file charges when the general outcry is great.

It has been said that the prosecutor should make justice "be seen publicly as being done." The public respect for the judicial process will in no small way be affected by prosecutorial behavior. The prosecutor must decide if the public's regard for the law will be harmed if a man is brought to trial and is not convicted. Even the name of the offense may prejudice a jury in favor of acquittal. F. A. Walterskirchen, President Judge of the King County Superior Court, commented:

> "When negligent homicide was called manslaughter, we found that the average juror thought the idea repugnant—the name of the crime chilled him. He was usually very reluctant to bring in a guilty plea. At the same time we had to remember that we had a high number of traffic deaths and needed to do something to reduce them."

Cates suggests that "too many acquittals are bound to call into question respect for law and the validity of the process of the courts."[28] Is it better to let a guilty man go free than to attempt a prosecution which is bound to fail?

The cost of expending organization resources may be a reason for withholding prosecution. If the matter is trivial or if the accused must be extradited from another state, the costs may be considered too high to warrant action. There are also occasions when the accused is on parole, or has a prior deferred or suspended sentence.

> "Depending upon the charge, there is no need to start prosecution. If, for instance, it is robbery, don't spend time and money before a judge prosecuting the case, just go up [to a judge] and get the parole revoked."

Organizational influences on the decision to prosecute are many. Certainly the exchange relationships between the police and the prosecutor, congestion within the judicial system, and community pressure are factors which are considered at this juncture. The prosecutor must decide which charge is appropriate to the facts of the case, the needs of the defendant, and the needs of society. He may decide to "throw the book" at the defendant, only to have it boomerang when he is unable to prove his case in court. He may charge the defendant with serious or multiple offenses to increase his latitude in plea bargaining.

Actions Other Than Prosecution

Respondents estimated that over 90 percent of the cases brought to the prosecutor's office by the police are filed in justice court for a preliminary hearing. Since little is known about the case at this point other than the information in the police report, the preliminary hearing affords the prosecutor an opportunity to see the evidence and hear the witnesses for the first time. As mentioned earlier, there are occasions when the prosecutor will not file charges but will take some other action to dispose of a case. In some instances the prosecutor may merely refuse the police request to issue a warrant; in others he may use another tactic which, although it does not result in prosecution, may satisfy the complainant and the public.

If there has been a violation of vice codes, the prosecutor may institute padlocking proceedings to abate the nuisance, thus making further action unnecessary. Such an action shifts attention from the offender to the owner of the property, who may, but usually does not, contest the action.

"The New Richmond Hotel was a whore house that wasn't being run right. You have to keep a professional madam to run a place like that—keep the girls in line, keep the bums out. The police will leave them alone if things are orderly. Well, they started having fights and knifings there . . . so the place was padlocked. It was a bad situation that needed cleaning up."

Restitution may be sought as an alternative to prosecution in bad check, embezzlement, and fraud cases. In the King County office a form letter is sent to those accused of writing "insufficient funds checks," asking them to "come in to talk things over." Through this method the check writer is induced to make restitution, without the necessity of formal charges. Although he has a responsibility to act in these situations, Carroll feels that he must guard against the use of his office as a collection agency. Complainants must show a willingness to file formal charges if mediation does not bring results.

If the prosecutor feels that another governmental agency is better equipped to handle a case, he may refer it. Some cases are sent to the corporation counsel or to the United States attorney. Welfare agencies may be asked to assume the responsibility where marital or medical difficulties seem to be at the root of the accused's problem.

Within the context of the legal system the prosecutor has freedom to find alternatives to the formal process. During the initial phase, when information upon which to base a judgment is scarce, evidential or other surface considerations are important. Prior to filing charges, the prosecutor is engaged in exchange relationships primarily with official agencies, although community influentials and defense counsel are sometimes active. A cardinal rule of prosecution seems to be "Don't discuss the case with counsel until it is filed in court." After the preliminary hearing a continuation may be sought, during which negotiations for a lesser charge become the overriding consideration of both prosecutor and defense counsel.

THE OFFICE AS A POLITICAL STEPPINGSTONE

Since the Cleveland Crime Survey when Roscoe Pound, Felix Frankfurter, and Raymond Moley found that interest groups and party politics were involved in criminal law, the office of the prosecuting attorney has been viewed as a steppingstone to higher office. There has been the belief that the typical prosecutor attains the office early in his legal career, holds it for only a short period, then uses it to attain the public attention necessary to be elected to higher office.

In recent years the activities of New Orleans Prosecutor Jim Garrison and those of Edmund Denis, District Attorney of Dukes County, Massachusetts, have again drawn attention to the political potentialities of the office. Garrison's attempt to overturn the Warren Commission's findings through the indictment of Clay Shaw might have led to his dramatic political advancement in the hurly-burly of Louisiana politics had he been more successful. Likewise, the persistence by which Denis, who had lost the Democratic nomination for United States senator in 1960, reopened the case against Senator Edward Kennedy has many of the characteristics associated with the factionalism of Massachusetts politics.

On first glance it would seem natural that the prosecutor's office would act as a powerful base from which to launch a quest for public position. Because he deals with dramatic, sensational material, the prosecutor can create a favorable climate of public opinion through the communications media. His discretionary powers may be used so that voters will be impressed with his abilities, charges may be dropped to avoid difficult cases, investigations may be initiated at politically opportune times, and disclosures may be made of suspected wrongdoing by members of the opposition. Jacob and Vines write that the discretionary powers often "allow him to become a key figure in the local political machine."[29]

Although the examples of successful prosecutor-politicians are numerous, the description of the office as a steppingstone has come into question. As several political scientists have noted, one can cite many areas of the country where the record of upward mobility from the prosecuting attorney's office is unimpressive. In Illinois, for instance, the sole person to win the governorship from a "law enforcement" background was Dwight H. Green, who as a United States attorney had prosecuted Al Capone for income tax evasion.[30] Jacob found that in Wisconsin the majority of prosecutors returned to private practice, their public office being only an interlude to promote "their career but not to launch themselves into political life."[31]

Weight must also be given to the fact that the office of prosecutor may itself be so important locally that there are few other equally worthwhile choices for a prosecutor. A "career prosecutor," such as Frank Hogan, who has been in the New

York County office since 1942, may regard his position as a terminal office because of the importance of the rewards he receives from the political system. The fact that Hogan succeeded Dewey, whose crusading zeal led him to the governorship, may suggest that personal ambition is an important factor in the steppingstone thesis.

Only recently have social scientists begun to consider some of the variables which may account for differences in the career patterns of public officials. Although the subject abounds with "folk wisdom" concerning the type of office thought to be politically advantageous and the conditions to be faced on the road to the governor's mansion, little of a systematic nature has been written to attempt to examine the hypotheses.[32] Exceptions may be found in the various studies of the social backgrounds of decision makers, but these tend to present data outside a theoretical framework. Further, they relate personal characteristics to the actor's current position, without viewing the longitudinal nature of career development patterns. Perhaps one of the problems in this area is the elusiveness of the characteristics of the political career: the fact that social interactions define a career and must be identified both within and outside institutions.

In the State of Washington there are a number of prosecutors who have achieved higher elected office in the classic manner. Forty-two percent of the governors from 1870 to 1950 came directly from law enforcement positions. Both United States Senators Magnuson and Jackson and three of the five male congressmen have held prosecution offices. Among the leaders of state government, the 1968 Democratic gubernatorial nominee Attorney General John O'Connell had achieved public notice as prosecuting attorney of Pierce County by his campaign to end vice operations attracted by Fort Lewis Army Post. There are, however, a greater proportion of former prosecutors who have achieved positions in the judiciary. Of the twenty-one judges of King County Superior Court, more than half were introduced to the legal process through positions in the prosecutor's office. Among members of the minor judiciary the proportion is just as high. Still, there are persons such as

King County Prosecutor Carroll who have made a career of the office, remaining even when opportunities were presented for advancement.[33]

SUMMARY

Although a prosecutor is free from statutory checks on his power he must make decisions within an organizational framework and is thus subject to the influence of other actors. Because the legal system requires that a number of officials participate in decisions concerning the disposition of each case, bargaining occurs among the actors. The prosecutor—as a link between the police and the courts—holds a strategic position in this regard because all cases must pass through his office. Accordingly, he is able to regulate not only the flow of cases, but also the conditions under which they will be processed. Given the caseload which inundates the contemporary legal system and the scarcity of resources to deal with it, officials are pressed to dispense justice efficiently. The prosecutor's influence over other actors is based on these stresses within the environment. In addition, there is a dramatic aspect to his work which can be utilized to command public attention as a weapon against the police, the courts, or other actors who do not cooperate with the prosecutor's efforts.

Besides the power which a prosecutor may develop from the organization needs of his office, his political partisanship may enhance his status. Often he is able to mesh his own ambitions with the needs of his party and office. For instance, the appointment and utilization of deputies may serve the party's desire for new blood and the prosecutor's need for young lawyers. Also, the prosecutor may press charges in ways which enhance his own and his party's power. Cases may be processed so that few come to trial, and hence help to maintain the prosecutor's conviction record; investigations may be initiated before elections to embarrass the opposition; and charges may be pressed against public officials for political gain. More important, however, is the fact that certain groups and persons may not receive equal justice because of the prosecutor's determinations. The decision to prosecute is one of the more obvious arenas for the infusion of politics into the administration of criminal justice.

The state of social science research concerning the office of prosecuting attorney does not allow us to generalize from the case study presented above. What is known is that variations in modes of decision-making occur in other cities. Thus, McIntyre has written about judicial dominance of the charging process in Chicago,[34] and Castberg found that party politics was not important in the Illinois office he studied.[35] We know very little about this most important office in the criminal justice system.

NOTES

1. Lewis Mayers, *The American Legal System* (New York: Harper and Row, 1955), 411..

2. In various states the office is titled: District Attorney, Commonwealth's Attorney, Circuit Attorney, State's Attorney, County Attorney, Solicitor.

3. Raymond Moley, *Politics and Criminal Prosecution* (New York: Minton, Balch and Company, 1929), 78.

4. Donald Matthews, *U.S. Senators and Their World* (Chapel Hill: University of North Carolina Press, 1960), 35.

5. Joseph Schlesinger, *How They Became Governor* (East Lansing: Governmental Research Bureau of Michigan State University, 1957), 77.

6. Ernst Freund, *Administrative Powers over Persons and Property* (Chicago: University of Chicago Press, 1928), 20.

7. U.S., National Commission on Law Observance and Enforcement, *Reports* (1931), Number 4, *Prosecution.*

8. Mayers, 411.

9. Morris Ploscowe, "The Significance of Recent Investigations for the Criminal Law and Administration of Criminal Justice," University of Pennsylvania Law Review, 100 (April, 1952), 824.

10. *Commonwealth* v. *Margiotti* 325 Pennsylvania 17, 188 Atl 524 (1936).

11. Morris Ploscowe, *Crime and Criminal Law* (New York: Collier and Son, 1939), 194. An exception is Wisconsin, where statutes provide that the prosecuting attorney does not have to indict in assault and battery or disorderly conduct cases. See: "Statutory Discretion of the District Attorney in Wisconsin," Wisconsin Law Review (1953), 170-176.

12. Walter Lippmann, *A Preface to Morals* (New York: Macmillan, 1929), 279.

13. Carroll was defeated for re-election in 1970, after having served twenty-two years as prosecutor.

14. Herbert A. Simon, "Decision-Making and Administrative Organization," Public Administration Review, 4 (1944), 25.

15. G. Clinton Fogwell, "Yes, But Don't Stay Too Long," The Shingle, 10 (1957), 139.

16. *1958 Supplement to Lawyers in the United States: Distribution and Income* (Chicago: American Bar Foundation, 1959), 54-55.

17. Robert K. Merton, *Social Theory and Social Structure* (rev. ed.; New York: Free Press, 1957), 387-420; Alvin W. Gouldner, "Cosmopolitans and Locals," Administrative Science Quarterly, 2 (December, 1957-March, 1958), 281-306, 444-480.

18. Brian Grosman, *The Prosecutor* (Toronto: University of Toronto Press, 1969), 89.

19. Jerome Skolnick, *Justice Without Trial* (New York: John Wiley, 1966), 120.

20. U.S. President's Commission on Law Enforcement and Administration of Justice, *The Challenge of Crime in a Free Society* (1967), 128.

21. Edward Banfield, *Political Influence* (New York: Free Press, 1961), 264.

22. Daniel M. Ogden, Jr., and Hugh A. Bone, *Washington Politics* (New York: New York University Press, 1960), 69.

23. Robert F. Kennedy, *The Enemy Within* (New York: Harper, 1960), 9-14.

24. Ibid., 33n.

25. *ABF: Survey*, 5, 27.

26. Ithiel deSola Pool, Robert P. Ableson, and Samuel L. Popkin, *Candidates, Issues and Strategies* (Cambridge: M.I.T. Press, 1964), 21.

27. John Kaplan, "Prosecutorial Discretion—A Comment," Northwestern University Law Review, 60 (1965), 174.

28. Aubrey M. Cates, Jr., "Can We Ignore Laws?—Discretion Not to Prosecute," Alabama Law Review, 14 (1961), 6.

29. Herbert Jacob and Kenneth Vines, "The Role of the Judiciary in American State Politics," *Judicial Decision Making*, Glendon Schubert, ed. (New York: Free Press, 1963), 249.

30. Matthew Holden, Jr., and James B. Wood, "The Politics of Prosecution: A Bibliographic Working Paper" (mimeographed; Department of Political Science, University of Pittsburgh, 1966).

31. Herbert Jacob, *Justice in America* (Boston: Little, Brown, 1965), 78.

32. Joseph A. Schlesinger, *Ambition and Politics: Political Careers in the United States* (Chicago: Rand McNally, 1966), But see: Richard L. Engstrom, "Political Ambitions and the Prosecutorial Office," Journal of Politics, 33 (1971), 190.

33. Carroll was defeated by fellow-Republican Christopher Bayley in 1970. He, along with a number of public officials, was indicted by a county grand jury in July, 1971, on charges that they conspired to protect gambling and other illegal activities.

34. Donald M. McIntyre, "Study of Judicial Dominance of the Charging Process," Journal of Criminal Law, Criminology and Police Science, 59 (1968), 463.

35. Anthony D. Castberg, "Prosecutorial Discretion: A Case Study" (unpublished Ph.D. dissertation, Northwestern University, 1968).

ATTORNEYS FOR

THE DEFENSE

"Necessity has no law; I know some attorneys of the same."
—Poor Richard

"I have for announcement the opinion and judgment of the Court in Number One Fifty-five, Gideon against Wainwright," began Justice Hugo Black on March 18, 1963, as he read the opinion of the Supreme Court in one of the landmark cases of the century.[1] In its decision the Court ruled that defendants in state criminal trials had a right to counsel as provided by the Sixth Amendment through the Fourteenth. Although earlier cases had developed the guarantee of counsel in state capital trials and for those defendants in "special" circumstances, the case of Clarence Gideon allowed the Court to extend this right to indigents charged with felonies and serious misdemeanors. As the opinion notes:

"From the very beginning, our state and national constitutions and laws have laid great emphasis on procedural and substantive safeguards designed to assure fair trials before impartial tribunals in which every defendant stands equal before the law. This noble ideal

cannot be realized if the poor man charged with crime has to face his
accusers without a lawyer to assist him."

If the Supreme Court's interest in counsel for the poor had
stopped with the Gideon decision, we might ask questions
about the designation of the case as a landmark. As has been
shown before, the organizational context of criminal justice
would not be much influenced if indigents did not obtain the
use of counsel until they had arrived at the trial stage.

Clarence Gideon was certainly not typical of the defendants
processed through the lower courts of this country. In fact, his
story, told with the skill of court watcher Anthony Lewis,
makes one of the more exciting books ever written on American
justice.[2] Having been through the criminal justice system
many times, Gideon had educated himself on the due process
rights with the zeal and interest of a "prison lawyer." When
brought before the Circuit Court of Bay County, Florida, on a
charge of breaking into the Bay Harbor Poolroom, Gideon
refused to plead guilty, and asked the court to appoint counsel.
His request was denied. Upon conviction, which was affirmed
by the Supreme Court of Florida, Gideon filed an appeal, *in
pauperis,* to the United States Supreme Court.

The major question facing judicial administrators after the
Gideon decision was, "At what point must counsel be provided?" This was soon answered when, in the decisions made in
Escobedo vs. *Illinois* (1964) and *Miranda* vs. *Arizona* (1966), it
was ruled that the defendant has a right to counsel at the
stationhouse, when an investigation is no longer a general
inquiry but has begun to focus on a particular suspect. The rules
laid down in *Miranda* may be viewed as a code of conduct for
police investigators. They are now required to advise a person
held in custody of his rights, especially that he will be provided
with counsel. As Chief Justice Warren noted, "Our aim is to
assure that the individual's right to choose between silence and
speech remains unfettered throughout the interrogation process. . ."[3]

These five-to-four decisions of the Court set off a wave of
criticism from the police and other law enforcement officials.
Many claimed that with a lawyer present the police would be

unable to interrogate suspects effectively and that the number of confessions would diminish. Much of the recent political rhetoric concerning "law and order" seems based on the notion that the Court has thrown roadblocks in the way of the police, contributing to a rising crime rate. What Chief Justice Warren has made clear is that the Court was alarmed by the disparity between the treatment received by the rich and that received by the poor at the lower levels of the American justice system. As he said, "Justice will be universal in the country when the processes as well as the doors of the courthouse are open to everyone."[4]

Presumably the Court assumes that the process will become open when the adversary, combative aspects of the system are strengthened. This need for counsel was forcefully expressed by the Supreme Court almost forty years ago in the famous Scottsboro Case:

> "The right to be heard would be, in many cases, of little avail if it did not comprehend the right to be heard by counsel. Even the intelligent and educated layman has small and sometimes no skill in the science of law. . . ."[5]

This view has been repeated numerous times by the Court. Not only is counsel necessary in the courtroom, but assistance is required throughout the process. Even when a case does not get to the trial stage, counsel is important both to the defendant in plea bargaining and to the judge in recommending a just solution. Counsel may discover information about the defendant which would aid the court in maximizing the rehabilitative potential of the sentence.

Well-qualified and active defense counsel plays an essential role in keeping the system honest—the essence of the adversary system. Although his various precedural tactics will undoubtedly slow the disposition of cases, counsel is important as a conflict-causing stress in the administration of justice. Under ideal conditions his activity will spur the other actors in the system to "keep on their toes" so that they do not relax into the lethargy often associated with bureaucracy. As Martin Mayer has said, the presence of counsel means that "both police and prosecutor are more likely to require verification early in the game to support their inner conviction that this particular s.o.b. is guilty."[6]

Reinforcement of the adversary model will be realized only if the social and organizational setting enhances the role of the criminal lawyer. Merely to require the provision of counsel will not help if the attorney provided is ill-educated, poorly paid, and coopted by the administrative values of the system. Rather than act as the adversary challenging the decisions made throughout the process, defense counsel may, in fact, play the role of broker among the defendant, prosecutor, and judge. It is possible that a defendant with an attorney who is in tune with the system will be less of an impediment to the smooth operation of the administrative machine than would be the accused without a lawyer. The latter may be unwilling to cooperate because he does not understand the process. The assistance of counsel may help to "pull the loose ends together" so that a bargain can be worked out. In whose interest the bargain is made remains an open question.

Traditionally the criminal lawyer has been caught between divergent conceptions of his position. On one hand, the "Perry Mason" image views the defense attorney as involved in a "constant searching and creative questioning of official decisions and assertions of authority at all stages of the process."[7] However, he is also seen by the public as one who is somehow "soiled" by his clients—a fixer engaged in shady practices so that he may free his criminal clients from the rightful demands of the law. It would appear that although Perry Mason remains a folk hero, the public acts in accordance with the more tarnished image.

The public's assumption is probably an accurate reflection of the life styles of many lawyers engaged in criminal practice in large urban areas. Surrounding most metropolitan courthouses can be found the offices of lawyers such as those referred to as the "Fifth Streeters" in the District of Columbia and the "Clinton Street Bar" in Detroit. These designations refer to that group within the legal profession often found prowling the urban criminal courts searching for clients who can pay a modest fee. Some have referral arrangements with policemen, bondsmen, and other minor officials. Rather than prepare their cases for disposition through the adversary process, they negotiate guilty pleas and try to convince their clients that they have received exceptional treatment. Such lawyers cease to be true professionals, but instead act as fixers for a fee. They exist in a relatively closed system where there are great pressures to process large numbers of cases for small fees and depend upon the cooperation of judicial officials. This small group of practitioners is usually poorer educated, works harder, and is in a more precarious financial situation than are their brothers in corporate practice.

It is true that there are a number of nationally known attorneys such as Melvin Belli, F. Lee Bailey, and Edward Bennett Williams who have built reputations by adhering to the Perry Mason model. But these counselors are few, expensive, and usually take only the dramatic, widely publicized cases. They are not usually found at the county courthouse level. In addition, there are attorneys in the major metropolitan areas who are retained by criminal elements. As Llewellyn has pointed out, specialization will produce counter-specialization. The proficient criminal will seek a well-trained criminal specialist as his attorney.[8]

Between the polar types of a Melvin Belli and a member of the "Fifth Streeters," lies a large number of general practitioners who are willing, on occasion, to take criminal cases. Often they are members of or connected to a larger firm whose upper-status client has run afoul of the law. Although this group is fairly large, its members have little experience in trial work and do not have well-developed relationships with the actors in the criminal justice system. Lacking this inside know-how, they may find that their client is better served if a courtroom regular is given the case.

The Supreme Court's requirement that adequate counsel be provided came at a time when there was already an acute shortage of lawyers willing to take criminal cases. As the President's Commission noted, "The most vexing question in connection with increased provision of defense counsel is:

problems related to the provision of counsel to the poor. Yet it should also be stressed that the borderline indigent—the person with a low income but above the indigency test—may have to go heavily into debt to protect himself.

Under ideal conditions, we might hope that well-qualified counsel would be appointed early in the process and that he would pursue each case with zeal in the best adversary tradition. Yet as J. Edward Lumbard, chief judge of the United States Court of Appeals for the Second Circuit, notes, too often the right to counsel is mocked by the assignment of a lawyer in the courtroom, a brief conference with the defendant, followed by a plea of guilty.[32] It is this aspect, the quality of counsel, which is a major concern of those hoping to instill due process values into the criminal justice system. As we have seen, the adversary elements can be emphasized only if there are incentives for counsel to defend an indigent with the same skill and vigor he brings to bear for a client who is paying his own bill.

Although the Court required counsel in the Gideon decision, it did not set standards for indigency. This concept has been variously defined throughout the country, with the ability to make bail often used as a sign that the defendant is able to afford counsel. This means that the defendant must choose between freedom before trial and an attorney. Remaining in jail can have serious effects on the accused's ability to hold his job and maintain stability within his family. Even with the widespread judicial knowledge of the Supreme Court's rule on counsel there are some parts of the country where the indigent are not given a lawyer unless the charge is sufficiently serious.

In the United States there are two basic methods through which counsel is provided indigent defendants—assigned counsel, where the attorney is appointed by the court to represent a particular defendant, and the use of a defender system in which a public official is counsel for the indigent. Although the defender system is growing rapidly, there are approximately 2,750 of the 3,100 counties which use the assigned-counsel approach. Especially in rural areas where the crime rate is low, assigned counsel is the usual method. But surprisingly there are some large cities still using assigned counsel, or a combination of the two methods. Within these two broad categories there are variations. In Illinois, for example, there is the so-called "mixed" system in which the state provides counsel, but a lawyer may be assigned under certain circumstances. Each system has its advantages and disadvantages, which have been endlessly argued in the law journals.

The assigned-counsel plan lends itself to two methods of appointment. In some cities the judges select attorneys by using a system of strict rotation from a list of lawyers submitted by the local bar association. This often means that the younger attorneys are called upon to perform this service as a civic and professional duty. In Houston, however, all four thousand lawyers in Harris County who are under fifty are available for appointment. Thus, under ideal conditions, there is a possibility that some of the best and most prestigious lawyers will be found in the criminal courts. Proponents of the assignment method point out that it is inexpensive and results in an aggressive, well-planned defense by attorneys who want to uphold their reputations before the court and their peers. Through the chance of rotation, the method also means that some of the worst legal talent will appear as defense counsel. More important, critics have noted that lawyers will be appointed whose contact with the criminal law is limited to courses taken in law school. Since most bar association members rarely appear in court, some limiting their practice to real estate transactions, their knowledge of the criminal justice process is minimal.

In most urban areas which use the appointment system, the indigent bar is composed of attorneys who have indicated to the judge that they are willing to take cases. This can result in appointments limited to a small cadre of courtroom regulars who depend upon the small fees for their economic survival. Thus, only those lawyers who are unable to acquire other clients will volunteer for indigent service. As one Seattle judge noted, "It is only the recent law school graduates and old 'has beens' who are interested in these cases." Michael Moore found in his study of lawyers in Oregon that those appointed were younger, less experienced, and rated by other members of the bar as not so competent as retained counsel.[33]

In many cities the fee schedule for the defense of indigents may be an inducement for counsel to convince his client to plead guilty to a lesser charge. Until recent changes, the Seattle lawyer collected only the preparation fee of $25 when his indigent client pleaded guilty. It was more profitable for an attorney to handle a large number of cases on this basis than to spend an entire day in the courtroom, for which also he would receive only $25. One member of the Seattle bar had developed this practice to such a fine art that a deputy prosecutor said, "When you saw him coming into the office, you knew that he would be pleading guilty." Moore quotes a district attorney who thought that

> "counsel for indigents very often display an attitude of 'let's get it over with.' The same lawyer, whom I know to be a veritable tiger for a paying client, is in many cases a pussy cat when representing the indigent client. Such are the economic facts of life."[34]

The public defender is a twentieth-century response to the legal needs of the indigent. First started in Los Angeles County in 1914, the system has rapidly spread to a number of populous cities, as well as to some states such as Minnesota and Connecticut. Defender systems are currently operating in 272 counties having almost one-third of all felony defendants in the country.[35] Although initially funded from public and private sources (especially the Ford Foundation), most of the costs of criminal defense have been gradually assumed by government. Because the defender is a salaried employee, like the doctor in a municipal hospital, the provision of his services is a break with the traditional notion of a private professional serving individual clients for a fee.

Like many public employees, the defender is often overworked and underpaid. The public defender in Cook County, Illinois, operates with only thirty-nine attorneys, compared with one hundred sixty-six in Los Angeles County. The Chicago defenders are paid between $7,200 and $15,600, thus are primarily young men.[36]

.As distinguished from the assigned-counsel plan, the defender is an on-going participant in the criminal justice process. This fact is either hailed or damned by commentators on the system. Because the defender deals with only criminal cases, proponents claim that he is able to develop an expertise and continuity which is lacking under assigned counsel. In addition, most public defenders' offices include staff members who assist in the preparation of cases; work usually left to the private practitioner when the assignment system is utilized. In many cities where a defender office exists, it is often necessary to supplement its services with the appointment of private attorneys.

Critics point out that the defender's independence is undermined by his daily contact with the prosecutor and judge. While retained counsel has brief, businesslike encounters in the courtroom, the public defender "attends to the courtroom as his regular work place and conveys in his demeanor his place as a member of its core personnel."[37] Thus, he arrives at his station, the defense table, in the morning with his case files for the day, temporarily leaving his post when a private attorney's case is called. Since he is part of a functioning court system, the needs of the client may be relegated to a secondary consideration. This may mean that, although counsel is provided, the bureaucratic pressures of the system will overcome the desired adversary values. The behavior of the public defender may help to facilitate the prosecutor's needs so that the guilty plea is readily given and trial avoided. As the noted criminal lawyer Edward Bennett Williams has said:

> "The public defender and the prosecutor are trying cases against each other every day. They begin to look at their work like two wrestlers who wrestle with each other in a different city every night and in time get to be good friends. The biggest concern of the wrestlers is to be sure they do not hurt each other too much. They don't want to get hurt. They just want to make a living."[38]

Social scientists who have compared the assigned counsel and defender approaches do not seem to have developed the evidence which can definitively support one system over the other. Analysis of their work requires that one acknowledge certain value judgments and specific criteria which serve as indices. Does the early appointment of counsel really make a difference in the quality of the defense? Is the proportion of clients pleading guilty an indication that one type of defense system is better than another?

The limited number of case studies of various justice systems precludes comparative statements since the data are produced from different processes with rules which vary greatly. Thus local norms concerning the determination of indigency, the point at which counsel is selected, and the caseload pressure on a particular system can greatly influence the effectiveness of an attorney. Oaks and Lehman, for instance, found that in Cook County the public defender generated more guilty pleas than did those lawyers who had been either privately retained or assigned to cases.[39] Yet the possibility exists that these differences may only reflect the types of defendants associated with each category of counsel. As previously shown, a major portion of the criminal defendants in any city will be poor. This can mean that the public defender will be handling cases for clients charged with crimes such as assault or robbery which reflect his social environment and status. "For every Speck case, the public defender gets thousands of impoverished defendants who have committed unspectacular crimces without imagi-nation or style."[40] Retained counsel may serve upper-status defendants who are charged with "white collar" crimes which are more difficult to detect and prosecute. In addition, there is a great possibility that the defender serves individuals with prior records who will probably receive a lighter sentence if a guilty plea is arranged.

David Neubauer found, using Silverstein's national survey data, that the public defender is appointed earlier, disposes more quickly the cases of defendants not released on bail, and achieves shorter jail terms for his clients.[41] On the other hand, he found that the public defender and assigned counsel systems were similar in their ability to provide counsel for indigents, to secure a defendent's release on bail, and to bargain with the prosecutor. Perhaps the rhetoric of the debate in the law journals has been meaningless. As Silverstein concludes, "No firm conclusions can be drawn as to whether assigned counsel systems are better than defender systems, or vice versa."[42] Oaks and Lehman note with some regret the trend toward greater reliance upon the public defender. They recommend the continuation of both types of counsel, since each contributes in specific ways to the effectiveness of the criminal justice system.

DEFENSE COUNSEL IN THE EXCHANGE PROCESS

We have seen that most of the criminal lawyers in metropolitan courts are persons whose professional environment is precarious. In a judicial system where bargaining within an administrative context is a primary method of decision-making, it is not surprising that defense attorneys find it essential to maintain close personal ties with the police, prosecutor, and other court officials. Thus the ability of the attorney to establish and continue a pattern of informal personal relations with these individuals is essential both for his own professional survival and for the opportunity to serve the needs of his clients. At every step of the criminal process, from the first contact with the accused, until final disposition of the case, the defense attorney is dependent upon decisions made by other judicial actors. Even such seemingly minor activities as visiting the defendant in jail, learning the case against him, and setting bail can be made difficult by these officials unless cooperation by the defense is maintained.

Criminal lawyers studied in Seattle were quite open in revealing their dependence upon personal relationships with decision makers. Wood found that 80 percent of the criminal lawyers he observed believed that friendly relations with the police were important, while 57 percent also felt that contacts with the prosecutor were very desirable.[43] This needs further examination, given our understanding of the central role of the prosecutor in the system. Comments elicited from the respondents noted that although the prosecutor was a key to plea bargaining, the police were also significant since they may misconstrue the facts of arrest, send clients to favored attorneys, and recommend lesser charges to the prosecutor.

There is a tendency for former deputy prosecutors to enter the practice of criminal law. Because of their "inside" knowledge of procedures in the prosecutor's office and friendships with court officials, they feel that they have an advantage over other criminal law practitioners. All of the former deputies interviewed in Seattle said that they took criminal cases. Of the eight criminal law specialists, seven had served as deputy prosecutors in King County, while the other was prosecuting attorney in a neighboring county.

We should not assume that counsel is at the complete mercy of judicial actors. At any phase of the process, the defense has the ability to invoke the adversary model with its formal rules and public battle. It is this potential for a trial with its expensive, time-consuming, and disputatious features which the effective counsel can use as a bargaining tool with the police, prosecutor, and judge. A well-known tactic, certain to raise the ante in the bargaining process, is for the defense to ask for a trial and to proceed as if they meant it.

Not only does the public trial create additional uncertainties for all the actors, but the requirements of evidence and procedure make the work of both sides more difficult. In addition, the justice system operates like a small town. Because judicial personnel must interact on a continuing basis, efforts are made to insure that personal relationships are cordial. The introduction of adversary tactics is disruptive of interpersonal relations; thus every effort is made to temper potential animosities for the benefit of the participants and to the possible detriment of the clients.

Some attorneys are able to play the adversary role with skill. They have developed a style which emphasizes the contentious behavior of a professional who is willing to fight the system for his client. Such lawyers are experienced in the courtroom and have built a practice around defendants who can afford the expensive costs entailed. Further, there may be clients who demand and expect their counsel to play the combatant role, feeling that they are not getting their money's worth unless verbal pyrotechnics are involved. The costs of this style of practice are not only financial. There must be willingness to gamble that the results of a trial will benefit the accused and counsel more than a bargain arranged with the prosecutor. Having broken the informal rules, the combative attorney may find that he is unable to obtain cooperation from the police and prosecutor in future relationships. As Grosman notes, they are subject to the "bare bones of the legal system."[44]

But for the criminal lawyer who depends upon a large volume of petty cases from clients who are poor and probably guilty, the incentives to bargain are strong. In his ability to secure cases, to serve his clients' interests, and to maintain his status as a practitioner, the criminal lawyer has found that friendship and influence with judicial officials is essential. The defense lawyer who is perceived to be part of the system may even be able to obtain full disclosure of the prosecution's case before trial. He, in return, agrees not to use this evidence for pre-trial cross-examination of prosecution witnesses and "is likely to enter a guilty plea after assessment of the prosecution's evidentiary strength."[45] Skolnick found that over 83 percent of the defense attorneys in his study of "Westville" insisted that the layman's notion of adversariness "was not in the interest of their clients and that clients did better as a result of a 'cooperative' posture."[46]

Securing Cases

Like other professions where the potential for client exploitation exists, the American bar has erected rigid strictures against the solicitation of clients. Lawyers are not allowed to advertise their services, and those with reputations as "ambulance chasers" soon find that their conduct is held in low regard by colleagues. Unlike their ties with members of the medical profession—which has similar canons—most citizens do not have a "family lawyer" and must seek out legal services in exceptional circumstances. This means that for both the practitioner trying to make a living and the accused who is in need of counsel, the difficulties of establishing contact may be severe.

There are possibly criminal lawyers who chase patrol wagons, but most depend on a broker—a person who by a "variety of circumstances is in a peculiarly advantageous or sensitive position for identifying and channelling potential legal business to the lawyer."[47] The broker may be a bondsman, police-man, fellow attorney, prison official, or social worker. The criminal lawyer seeking clients has the problem of making himself known to the broker and creating a climate so that cases will be referred. Active participation in social or political groups is one way the attorney makes contact with brokers. Favors, such as free legal advice on personal matters to law enforcement actors, can further the relationship. This arrangement for the funneling of clients can mean that the lawyer becomes obligated more to his broker than to his client. A police captain is probably going to be less likely to hand the attorney's business card to a prisoner if, on the basis of past experience, he has found that the lawyer is not cooperative. Unfortunately, defendants come and go, but the broker remains in his advantageous position.

Relations with Clients

If the criminal lawyer is not an advocate, using technical skills to win a case, what is the service which he performs for the accused? We have shown that one of the assets which he sells is his influence within the judicial system, his ability to bargain for the defendant. Underlying this emphasis is a second service which Blumberg has labeled the attorney's "agent-mediator" role.[48] In this capacity the criminal lawyer helps the accused to redefine his situation and to restructure his perceptions, and thus prepares the client to accept the consequences of a guilty plea. The interrelatedness of these services is evident; success in one venture is dependent upon success in the other. If a client balks at the bargain which has been struck, the attorney's future influence with the prosecutor may be jeopardized. At the same time, the lawyer does not want to get a reputation for selling out his clients, ad advertisement which may quickly end his career.

In the process of "cooling out" the accused, the lawyer is often assisted by the defendant's kin, probation officer, prosecutor, and judge. All try to emphasize that they want the accused to "do the right things for his own good." Thus the defendant finds himself in a position analogous to that of a patient where various treatments are urged upon him by those proclaiming that they are working in his interest.

The public defender has a special problem of client control. Since the defendant has not selected his counsel, he may balk at accepting the bargain, insisting that a trial be held. Because the public defender may fear a charge of misleading his client, he may have to invoke the formal procedure. The extent to which the defender *represents* the accused is open to question. Judicial actors may use the trial as an opportunity to impress upon other defendants the fact that a cooperative attitude is important.

The criminal lawyer acting as an agent-mediator may in fact be viewed as a double agent. With obligations to both his client and the court, he is a broker seeking to effect a satisfactory outcome. The position is filled with conflicts of interest. As Blumberg notes:

> "Too often these must be resolved in favor of the organization which provides him with the means of his professional existence. Consequently, in order to reduce the strains and conflict imposed in what is ultimately an overdemanding role obligation for him, the lawyer engages in the lawyer-client 'confidence game' so as to structure more favorably an otherwise onerous role system."[49]

The role of the defense attorney is structured by his occupational environment within the criminal justice system. Recruitment into criminal practice, financial considerations, interpersonal relations, and the demands of the system for a speedy disposition of a huge caseload create needs which are met through a process of bargaining. As a result, criminal lawyers participate in a number of exchange relationships which influence case disposition. A primary focus for decision-making is plea bargaining, where the various perspectives of the defendant, prosecutor, defense lawyer, and judge are brought to bear. As one judge told the author, "Lawyers are helpful to the system. They are able to pull things together, work out a deal, keep the system moving."

NOTES

1. Anthony Lewis, *Gideon's Trumpet* (New York: Random House, 1964), 187.

2. Ibid.

3. *Miranda* v. *Arizona* 384 U.S. 436 (1966).

4. Earl Warren, "The Advocate and the Administration of Justice in an Urban Society," 47 Texas Law Review 616 (1969).

5. *Powell* v. *Alabama* 287 U.S. 45 (1932).

6. Martin Mayer, *The Lawyer* (New York: Harper and Row, 1966), 158.

7. U.S., Attorney General, *Poverty and the Administration of Federal Criminal Justice,* 1963, 10.

8. Karl N. Llewellyn, "The Bar Specializes—With What Results?" Annals, 167 (May, 1933), 181.

9. U.S., President, Commission on Law Enforcement and Administration of Justice, *The Challenge of Crime in a Free Society,* 1967, 151.

10. B. James George, "The Imperative of Modernized Criminal Law Teaching," 53 Kentucky Law Review 461 (1965).

1. U.S., President, Commission on Law Enforcement, *Task Force Report: The Courts,* 55-56.

12. C. Wright Mills, *White Collar* (New York: Oxford, 1951), 122.

13. Samuel Untermyer, "What Every Present-Day Lawyer Should Know," Annals, 167 (1933), 173-176.

14. Walter I. Wardwell and Arthur L. Wood, "The Extraprofessional Role of the Lawyer," American Journal of Sociology, 61 (1956), 306.

15. Erwin O. Smigel, "Impact of Recruitment on the Organization of the Large Law Firm," American Sociological Review, 25 (1960), 55-60.

16. Jack Ladinsky, "The Impact of Social Backgrounds of Lawyers on Law Practice and the Law," Journal of Legal Education, 16 (1963), 128.

17. Everett C. Hughes, *Men and Their Work* (New York: Free Press, 1958), 71.

18. Ibid.

19. Ladinsky, 139.

20. Arthur Wood, *Criminal Lawyer* (New Haven: College and University Press, 1967), 54.

21. An exception is Abraham Blumberg, who found that the attorneys in "Metropolitan Court" differed from those criminal lawyers described by other social scientists. See: *Criminal Justice* (Chicago: Quadrangle Books, 1967), 108-110.

22. Jerome Carlin, *Lawyers on Their Own* (New Brunswick: Rutgers University Press, 1962); *Lawyers' Ethics* (New York: Russell Sage, 1966).

23. Ibid., 173.

24. Richard H. Kuh, "Careers in Prosecution Offices," Journal of Legal Education, 14 (1961), 179.

25. Blumberg, 110.

26. Mayer, 162.

27. Carlin, *Lawyers' Ethics*, 85.

28. John Crow, "A Professional's Dilemma: The Criminal Law" (unpublished manuscript).

29. Wood, 129.

30. Richard A. Watson and Rondal G. Downing, *The Politics of the Bench and the Bar* (New York: John Wiley, 1969).

31. Lee Silverstein, *Defense of the Poor* (Chicago: American Bar Foundation, 1965), 9-10.

32. J. Edward Lumbard, "The Adequacy of Lawyers Now in Criminal Practice," Journal of the American Judicature Society, 47 (1964), 176.

33. Michael Moore, "The Right to Counsel for Indigents in Oregon," 44 Oregon Law Review (1965), 255-300.

34. Ibid., 283.

35. President's Commission, *Task Force Report: The Courts*, 59.

36. Howard James, *Crisis in the Courts* (New York: McKay, 1968), 136.

37. David Sudnow, "Normal Crimes: Sociological Features of the Penal Code in a Public Defender Office," Social Problems, 12 (1965), 255-276.

38. Edward Bennett Williams, *The Law*. Interview by Donald McDonald (New York: Center for the Study of Democratic Institutions, n.d.), 10.

39. Dallin H. Oaks and Warren Lehman, *A Criminal Justice System and the Indigent* (Chicago: University of Chicago Press, 1968), 176.

40. Dallin H. Oaks and Warren Lehman, "Lawyers for the Poor," Transaction, 4 (1967), 26.

41. David Neubauer, "Counsel for Indigents' An Empirical Examination of the Criminal Court Process," paper read at the 1968 Annual Meeting of the American Political Science Association, Washington, D.C.

42. Silverstein, 73.

43. Wood, 156.

44. Brian Grosman, *The Prosecutor* (Toronto: University of Toronto Press, 196), 80.

45. Ibid., 76.

46. Jerome Skolnick, "Social Control in the Adversary System," Journal of Conflict Resolution, 11 (1967), 61.

47. Blumberg, 135.

48. Abraham Blumberg, "The Practice of Law as Confidence Game," Law and Society Review, 1 (1967), 11-39.

49. Ibid., 38-39.

COURTS

"Yet trial-court fact-finding is the toughest part of the judicial function. It is there that court-house government is least satisfactory. It is there that most of the very considerable amount of judicial injustice occurs. It is there that reform is most needed."[1]

The President's Commission expressed shock at the conditions found in the lower courts during its recent study:

"It has seen cramped and noisy courtrooms, undignified and perfunctory procedures, and badly trained personnel. It has seen dedicated people who are frustrated by huge caseloads, by the lack of opportunity to examine cases carefully, and by the impossibility of devising constructive solutions to the problems of offenders. It has seen assembly line justice."[2]

The commission was exposed to one of the major facts of life in the United States—the "law explosion." Because of an increased population, greater urbanization, and technological change, society is far more complex and vastly more demanding of law and legal institutions now than in its rural past.

The problem of court congestion has become widely recognized during the past decade. Governmental and lay groups have deplored the fact that defendants in criminal cases often wait in jail for months before they come to trial. The phrase "assembly line" justice is used by many to characterize the high percentage of guilty pleas, bargaining, and the absence of the due process version of criminal justice. Yet the conditions in the criminal courts point up the reality of the filtering effect, the administrative determination of guilt, and the exchange relationships which characterize the system. The additional judges and courtrooms demanded by reformers will not bring about the emphasis upon due process values as long as the system is able to function consistent with the needs of the players.

Given the emphasis of this book on pre-trial negotiations in the administration of justice, it might seem surprising that space should be devoted to judges and the courtroom. But of the many actors in the criminal justice process, it is the judge who is perceived as holding the greatest amount of leverage and influence over the system. Decisions of the police, defense attorneys, and prosecutor are greatly affected by his rulings and sentencing practices. Although we tend to think of the judge primarily in connection with the trial, his work is much more varied; he is a continuous presence throughout the activities leading to disposition of the case. Signing warrants, fixing bail, arraigning defendants, accepting guilty pleas, scheduling cases— all are portions of the judge's work outside the formal trial.

More than any other actor in the system, the judge is expected to embody the symbol of justice, insuring that due process rights are respected and that the defendant is fairly treated. He is supposed to act within and without the courthouse according to well-defined role prescriptions which are designed to prevent his involvement in activities which may place the judicial position into disrepute. Yet the pressures of today's justice system often mean that the ideals of the judge's position have been relegated to a back seat while the need to keep up a speedy disposition of cases takes priority.

Throughout the United States the inferior or lower criminal courts operate under a variety of names: justice court, recorder's court, district court, or magistrate's court. These may be classified into "courts of first instance" and "courts of general jurisdiction." Criminal courts of first instance have powers limited to arraignment of all cases, preliminary hearings involving crimes which must be adjudicated by a higher level, disposition of summary offenses, and, in some states, trial of persons accused of some misdemeanors.[3]

Courts of general jurisdiction have the power to try all types of cases. In large metropolitan areas it is common to have divisions specializing in different kinds of cases. These courts also have an appeals function, hearing those defendants who appeal decisions made at the inferior level. The fact that multiple judges are used means that scheduling is an important consideration, since judges are assigned on a rotational basis. To preclude the possibility that courtrooms may have sitting judges without cases—a common occurrence, given the opportunity to plead guilty in the middle of a trial—a "calendar man" is employed to insure that backup cases are available to fill the void.[4] Recognizing disparities in some courts among the sentencing proclivities of judges, defense attorneys evolve intricate strategies to try to insure that a judge sumpathetic to their client's cause will hear the case. The use of continuances and influence with the calendar man are ways to achieve this goal.

The existing literature leaves the impression that judges in the lower criminal courts are very different in socio-economic characteristics and operate in a different organizational environment from those manning upper courts. Smith and Blumberg describe the judges of "Central Sessions Court" as being elected to the bench, with a mean age of fifty-one years, graduates of part-time proprietary law schools, and primarily from upwardly mobile ethnic groups.[5] Unfortunately, most of the scholarly work on judicial decision-making has focused on the United States Supreme Court and a few state supreme courts. One has the impression that justices manning these positions are much better educated and come from upper-status backgrounds. Because of the place of their court in the judicial hierarchy, upper-court judges are more concerned with formal legal requirements. They do not work under the pressure of huge caseloads and the tensions of administering the criminal justice bureaucracy. In addition, they are able to view cases from a distance, being immune from the personal dynamics of the actors. This means that theirs are "sagelike, rather than bureaucratic and instrumental role performances."[6]

In most cities the criminal court judge occupies the lowest status in the judicial hierarchy. Lawyers and laymen alike do not accord him the prestige which is characteristic of the mystique usually surrounding members of the bench. Even his brethren who hear civil cases in the lower courts may look down on him. As in other professional relationships, the criminal trial judge's prestige may be influenced by the status of the defendant. As Blumberg notes, "He is so close to the publics served daily by the bench and bar that, while he may retain the charismatic flavor of the office, his reputation becomes tarnished and somewhat mundane."[7] Often he has assumed the bench directly from a criminal law practice before the same court. Yet with these liabilities we expect the trial judge to keep the plea bargaining process moving so that the entire system will not flounder, while at the same time emphasizing the values of the due process model.

Like patrolmen, lower-court judges have many of the attributes of street-level bureaucrats.[8] They are able to exercise discretion in the disposition of summary offenses without the constant supervision of higher courts and have wide latitude in fixing sentences. This is especially noticeable in courts of first instance where sentencing of order-maintenance cases is carried out in a hurried manner, usually without a record being kept of the session. Foote's description of the disposition of vagrancy and drunkenness cases in Philadelphia illustrates this point:

"As court adjourned at 11:24, this left 15 minutes in which to hear the remaining 55 cases. During that time the magistrate discharged 40 defendants and found 15 guilty and sentenced them to three months terms in the House of Correction.

"Four of these committed defendants were tried, found guilty and sentenced in the elapsed time of seventeen seconds from the time that the first man's name was called by the magistrate through the pronouncing of sentence upon the fourth defendant. In each of these cases the magistrate merely read off the name of the defendant, took one look at him and said, 'Three months in the House of Correction.' "[9]

Since minor offenses are seldom reviewed by higher courts, and the actual limits of vagrancy are set not in the statute but by the practices of the police and magistrates, discretion is the key variable.

Studies of criminal courts of first instance show that cases are handled in volume; all of the defendants charged with a particular offense are herded before the bench, the citation is read by the clerk, and sentences given by the judge. Foote observed one court which handled 1,600 summary cases a month, sometimes disposing of each defendant in less than one minute. Similar work has demonstrated that the courts in New York, Los Angeles, and Chicago operate in much the same fashion.[10] Although disposition of vagrancy cases probably is the most blatant examples of mass justice, other misdemeanors are often handled just as rapidly and with a similar disregard for due process. In Boston, observers for the Lawyers' Committee for Civil Rights Under Law concluded:

"All court personnel, defendants, and eventually the community—which because of the nature of the court's jurisdiction means the poor people within that community—come to recognize that the judge's personal power and personal prejudices overshadow established rules of law in the district courts."[11]

JUDICIAL SELECTION

The quality of justice depends to a great extent on the quality of the judges. Since government has been given the power to deprive an individual of his liberty or his life, good judges are essential. This need has been recognized in connection with the character and experience of those appointed to our highest courts. Less interest has been focused on trial judges, those persons who have the most contact with the public. Where judges are elected, only a small portion of the voters participate. In fact, a survey by the Institute of Judicial Administration shows that although over 80 percent of judicial positions in the United States are elective, about half those judges responding were initially appointed to fill vacancies occasioned by death or retirement.[12] In states where appointment governs selection, little effort is expended on examining the credentials of the nominees. In some states it is possible for a person with little or no legal training to be made a judge. This is an unsatisfactory situation, since the public's impression of the criminal justice system is shaped, to a great extent, by the trial judge's demeanor and the dignity he imparts to the courtroom.

> "When judges are rude or inconsiderate or permit their courtrooms to become noisy, crowded dispensaries of rapid-fire justice, public confidence in the fairness and effectiveness of the criminal process is diminished."[13]

Methods used to select judges have been a source of concern to advocates of reform. There are essentially five different methods used by various states: partisan election, non-partisan election, appointment by the governor, appointment by the legislature, and merit selection. Throughout all of the arguments advanced for one method or another, a persistent conflict appears regarding the desired qualities of a judge and the assumption that the type of selection process will enhance the propensities for different judicial styles. On the one hand is the view that the judge should be concerned only with the law, and on the other that he "must feel the pulse of the people in order to accomplish justice. . . ."[14] Whatever the rationale, the fact remains that different approaches enhance or diminish political opportunities for different individuals and interests.

Popular election of judges occurs in more than half the states, with nineteen using the partisan approach. This method has probably received the most criticism, since there is the belief that judgeships go only to those who have earned their robe through duty to the party. Yet this criticism is not uniform. The reformist American Judicature Society claims that political parties usually provide competent candidates and that is is from non-partisan elections where the voter is not guided by the party emblem that the worst judges emerge. As its editorial observes:

"Having the same name as a well-known public figure, a large campaign fund, a pleasing TV image, or the proper place on the ballot are far more influential in selecting judges than character, legal ability, judicial temperament or distinguished experience on the bench."[15]

In many cities judgeships provide "much of the fuel for party engines."[16] Because of the honorific and material rewards which may be gained from the position, political parties are able to secure the energy and money of those attorneys who view a judgeship as the capstone of a legal career. In addition, a certain amount of courthouse patronage may adhere to the position, since clerks, bailiffs, and secretaries—all jobs which may be filled with active party workers—are appointed by the judge. Given the hegemony of the Democratic party in cities such as New York and Chicago, selections for judicial posts are solely in the hands of political leaders. Since there are many candidates, it is often charged that money plays a primary role. Sayre and Kaufman have said that in New York the amount varies according to the humber of election districts included in the judicial area.[17] Others have noted that two years' salary is the going price. Yet New York County Democratic leader Edward Costikyan said that of the thirteen judgeships filled under him from 1962 to 1964, "In no case . . . was money a factor."[18] One hopes that cash is not being exchanged for judicial appointments, as it was during the 1930's, when the Seabury investigations reported that "payments were made in crisp, undeclared currency,"[19] yet one may suspect that more subtle means, like contributions to fund-raising benefits or "loans" to the party, are used. It should also be recognized that ethnic and religious characteristics may be important criteria; the balanced ticket is not confined to "political" offices. Judgeships may also be employed by party leaders to retire officials from the legislative or executive branches. For a variety of reasons, then, it is obvious that party fortunes figure importantly in judicial selection.

The Missouri Plan of selection on merit is a combination of appointment and election that was first instituted in 1940. When a judicial vacancy occurs, the nominating commission of laymen and attorneys for the affected bench sends the governor the names of three candidates, from among whom he selects the replacement. After a year a referendum is held to determine the judge's retention. Ten states now use this plan, which has been backed by groups such as the American Bar Association and the American Judicature Society. Designed to remove partisan politics from the judiciary, it is also supposed to have the advantage of giving the electorate an opportunity to remove sitting judges.

Despite the impressive support of bar groups, the Missouri Plan has not gone unchallenged. Many lawyers regard it as a system favoring the selection of "blue bloods," those attorneys with ties to corporations, to the detriment of the "little guy." As Watson and Downing have shown, the plan replaces party politics with bar politics. Under it, membership on the nominating commissions is a key to influence within the process. In both Kansas City and St. Louis, seats are competed for by rival organizations of attorneys representing the basic plaintiff-defendant cleavage in the profession and reflecting the social status, political affiliations, and types of practices within the bar.

> "The stakes of these elections for lawyers relate both to the perceived policy 'payoffs' in terms of judges' rulings that affect their clients' economic interests and to symbolic 'payoffs' for the contending bar groups involving matters of prestige and ideology."[20]

Although there has been extensive discussion regarding selection systems, little research has probed the cynamics and consequences of the several methods. Do they have class implications, as some believe? Do some favor the selection of politically oriented judges as opposed to legally oriented judges? If each has built-in biases, are these transmitted by the judges. actions to the criminal process?

If all lawyers are considered to be a potential pool for recruitment to judgeships, a winnowing process may operate so that some attorneys are separated out because of their own ambitions, financial situation, or background characteristics.

Given the availability of a person who has felt the "pull of the robe," his chances for success may rest on his visibility to significant actors. For example, in a system where judges are appointed by the governor, one must be visible to him either directly, or indirectly through persons or groups having influence with him.[21]

Political scientists have shown that the structure of government is often influenced by the socio-economic characteristics of the population.[22] Non-partisan elections, the city manager form of government, and other reforms tend to occur in cities with a large number of middle-class professionals, a low percentage of residents who are members of ethnic groups, and an economic structure which is more "white-" than "blue-" collar. In cities with a highly partisan political complexion the opposite appears to be true. Such communities tend to be heterogeneous, with a variety of ethnic and economic cleavages which are translated into political competition. Given these variables we should expect the process for recruiting judges to differ with the dominant political ethos as influenced by these population characteristics. Further, it might be expected that the attitudes of the judges from these cultures will reflect the dominant values of the community. Decisions in criminal cases may be viewed as an outcome of this complex of variables.

Jacob has conducted a study comparing judicial selection systems in twelve states.[23] His results show that appointment by the governor results in judges who are low on indices of localism and education. Not too surprisingly, a small proportion of those elected on a partisan basis held prior public or party office. This may imply that parties expect candidates for judgeships to have certain characteristics which will make the voter think that they are "above" politics. Nagel's work shows that judges who are Democrats tend to have greater sympathy for the defendant than do Republicans.[24]

Levin's comparison of the criminal courts of Pittsburgh and Minneapolis is the major study which seeks to relate selection methods to judicial decisions.[25] In Pittsburgh, judges are chosen through the highly politicized environment of a city controlled by the Democratic party.

"Public and party offices are filled by party professionals whose career patterns are hierarchical and regularized. They patiently 'wait in line' because of the party's need to maintain ethnic and religious 'balance' even on a judicial ticket."[26]

Partisan politics is so much a part of the culture than the public accepts the idea that the courts should be staffed with party workers. There has been little enthusiasm for efforts to reform the selection process.

Minneapolis has a system which is formally non-partisan; political parties have almost no place in the selection of judges, while the bar association plays an influential role. Minnesota governors have traditionally appointed judges according to the preference of the attorneys. This means that judicial candidates usually come from the large, business-oriented law firms and have not been active in partisan politics.

The differing selection methods and political milieus of these two cities lead to contrasting sentencing decisions in the criminal courts. In general, judges in Pittsburgh are more lenient that are those in Minneapolis. Not only do white and black defendants receive a greater percentage of probation and a shorter length of incarceration in Pittsburgh, but the pattern is maintained when the defendants' records, pleas, and ages are held constant, and the relationship holds true for the nine offenses compared.

Levin's analysis suggests that Minneapolis judges approximate a model of judicial decision-making which emphasized the facts developed through the adversary system. In addition, they stress the need to maintain an emotional distance from the defendant and to affirm the importance of procedures. By contrast Pittsburgh judges approximate the values of administrative decision-making where discretion is used to obtain a solution which is considered "just" even though it may be at variance with the formal rules. In many details these two models correspond with the values expressed in Packer's due process and criminal control orientations.

In the partisan environment of Pittsburgh, judges focus on the characteristics of the defendant and away from the formal dictates of the law. Their courtroom procedures are informal, so that decisions are based on intuition and impression.

"In their 'closeness' and 'empathy' with the defendant the Pittsburgh judges tend to stand apart from the law and to act as a buffer between it and the people upon whom it is enforced. They seek to 'help' the defendants, but they act as if their specific goal is achieving substantive justice and benevolence for the defendants rather than the 'rule of law' or 'legal justice.' "[27]

Compared to the defendant orientation of the Pittsburgh judge, those in Minneapolis are intent on protecting society. They tend to penalize defendants who plead not guilty by giving them more severe sentences. Minneapolis judges were asked by the Minnesota Department of Corrections to give the maximum sentences under the law so as to achieve uniformity throughout the state, giving prison officials more discretion in determining the exact dates of release. Levin reports that to a great extent the judges complied with this request. In sentencing, the nature of the charge and the defendant's prior record are more important considerations than details about his family life or social background characteristics.

The socialization and recruitment of judges seem to be an important influence on their decisions. The winnowing process may operate so that only certain types of persons who have had certain kinds of experiences are available for selection in each judicial system. Levin believes that any relationship between a judge's background and his decisions is indirect. What is crucial is the intervening variable of the city's political system and its influence on judicial selection, recruitment, and socialization.

Many observers believe that the quality of the judges manning the criminal courts is poor. The position of trial judge requires uncommon attributes of personality and character. Given the strains of an overloaded system it would seem to require skill and patience to deal with the daily problem of reducing the calendar while at the same time dispensing justice. Unfortunately, the President's Commission has said,

"there are judges, attorneys and other officers of the lower courts who are as capable as their counterparts in more prestigious courts, but the lower courts regularly do not attract such persons."[28]

COURTROOM INTERACTION

Although the traditional picture of the courtroom emphasizes the adversarial posture, a more realistic version might stress the fact that interactions among the major actors have many of the characteristics associated with those in a small group. To a significant degree the same prosecutors, judges, and defense attorneys find themselves in face-to-face contact, handling similar cases, month after month, with only the defendant changed. Accused persons pass through the system while court personnel remain, carrying on their careers and organizational enterprises. Individual cases may cause tensions, but these are generally overcome because of the larger need to preserve relationships so that interaction may be carried on in the future. The officers of the court have more in common, both in cultural values and goals, than any one of them shares with the defendant. Most have been socialized through law school to the norms of the legal profession. All share values which may be culturally different from those of the accused.

> "The client becomes a secondary figure in the court system as in other large organizational settings. He is a means to other, larger ends of the organization's incumbents. He may present doubts, contingencies, and pressures which challenge or disrupt existing informal networks, but they are usually resolved in favor of the organization."[29]

As noted throughout this book, it is in the interest of the three major actors in the courtroom drama to process most cases with the greatest amount of speed and efficiency and with the lowest risk to their personal goals. Judges are probably under less pressure from bureaucratic norms than are other participants in the criminal justice system, yet in actual practice they too feel the demands for efficiency and order. In multi-judge courts the judge who does not process his share of the workload may be socially ostracized by his brothers. Because he is often ill-equipped to handle the decision-making and administrative routine, the lower court judge must rely heavily on the services of others in the bureaucracy. As Smith and Blumberg note, new judges are " 'broken in' by clerks and other civil service functionaries will socialize them in terms of the 'practical' side of all the organizational features, goals and requirements. . . ."[30] In "Central Sessions Court" is was found that "regardless of their individual predilections, they learn to accept and internalize, for the most part, the routineering and ritualism of their socializers."[31]

An additional factor concerning judges may be that they feel more threatened by the gap between the due process values they have sworn to uphold and the reality of administrative decision-making. They may be anxious because the legal rules do not furnish adequate guidelines for their behavior. Even they must depend to a great extent on exchange relationships to maintain their position in the system and to meet the needs of a variety of actors and publics. This means that negotiations and efforts to minimize the adversarial nature are taken to insure that all will benefit. The exchange relationships of the pre-trial period continue as the defendant is brought before the court. The judge must play his part according to the script and not be inconsistent in his sentencing practices. This does not mean that he will enter directly into negotiations, but he may stop a trial, call the attorneys to the dais to ask, "Can't you get together on this?" Even for that small number of defendants who choose a trial by jury, the values of bargain justice may work a special twist, since those found guilty may receive harsher sentences for not following the norms of the system and pleading guilty.

The presentation of the actors on the courtroom stage illustrates the close relationships. Although the judge's bench is usually elevated, he is surrounded by bailiffs, clerks, and other supporting characters. Throughout the proceedings, lawyers from both sides periodically engage in muffled conversations with the judge out of the hearing range of defendant and spectators. Even the public defender, often representing as many as 90 percent of the clients, occupies a "permanent" place on the stage, momentarily relinquishing his desk to the few lawyers who have been privately retained.

"While the courtroom encounters of private attorneys are brief, businesslike and circumscribed, interactionally and temporally, by the particular cases that bring them there, the P.D. attends to the courtroom as his regular work place and conveys in his demeanor his place as a member of its core personnel."[32]

From the perspective of the defendant the adversarial stance must indeed appear to be fixed as these "agent-mediators"[33] decide his fate.

Suffet's study of bail setting in New York County Criminal Court is a good illustration of the social interactions among the judge, prosecutor, and defense. Although New York statutes specify the conditions for bail, norms emerge through courtroom interaction which guide the judge in determining the treatment of each defendant. Of the 1,473 bail settings observed, the judge made a decision in 49 percent without discussing the matter with the attorneys. Thirty-eight percent resulted from a suggestion as to bail by either the prosecutor or defense which was then accepted by the judge. In only 9 percent was there a conflict among the role players. The study showed that the prosecutor has more prestige in the courtroom than does the defense attorney, who was least likely to make the initial bail suggestion, and had the least chance of getting the judge to accede to it. Suffet found that the judge and prosecutor were mutually supportive and subscribed to the same bail standards.

The latent function of these bail setting interactions is to spread responsibility for release of the defendant, since judges are sensitive to public pressure. By including the other actors in the process he has an opportunity to create a "buffer between the court and the potential outraged response of the public to crimes which may be committed by persons at liberty pending court appearance."[35]

Another courtroom interaction which has an important effect on the outcome of the process is a request for continuance. Many judicial reform spokesmen cite this type of delay as crucial not only in slowing the court's work, but also because continuances often result in justice being denied. Banfield and Anderson's study of continuances in the Cook County Criminal Courts shows that guilty dispositions decrease as the number of court appearances increases.[36] Too often defendants with retained counsel are able to induce judges to delay a trial as a way of wearing out witnesses, of remaining out on bail as long as possible, or of waiting for community interest to die. These practices have the additional effect of discriminating in favor of those who can afford counsel. The poor, represented by the public defender, do not receive the same treatment.

Although exchange relationships in the courtroom influence decisions by the judge, prosecutor, and defense counsel, their effect touches other subsystems in the administration of justice. Cases which are dismissed by the judge may influence arrest practices since police may be reluctant to institute proceedings in similar future cases. Sentences given in court help attorneys and defendants to plan strategies. Prosecutors may *nolle pros.* certain cases because of their expected fate before the judge.

Blumberg has described the criminal court as a communication system in which the label "criminal" is fastened onto the guilty.[37] At the same time, it is a meeting place for "free professionals" who work in the service of the accused, supposedly to treat his needs and those of society. Yet even the professional skills of these actors are utilized only within the organizational context. For those who do not play the game according to the bureaucratic rules, various sanctions may be imposed: lawyers may find that they are unable to get favors from the prosecutor or judge, probation officers may be labeled "trouble makers," and the court psychiatrist's motives may be questioned. In addition, efforts are often made to bind members to the organization through complicity: shortcuts, unethical practices, and other "work crimes" may tie the prosecutor, defense attorney, clerk, and even judge to the norms of the bureaucracy from which one dares not deviate without the threat of exposure.

PLEA BARGAINING

"How to 'Settle' a Criminal Case" is the title of an article by Robert Polstein in a publication of the American Law Institute.[38] He points out that generally it is in the best interest of the defendant, his counsel, and the prosecutor to "settle" a case so that it does not result in a trial. "The widely held opinion that prosecutors never bargain is a myth," he says. It is true that they do not like to use the word "bargain," since they fear that the public will not understand the usefulness of negotiations. To protect his public record of success in achieving convictions, to expedite the work load of his office, and to cooperate with other actors in the system, the prosecutor is usually willing to reduce a charge in exchange for a guilty plea. Likewise, judges faced with an overloaded calendar and a complicated case will often urge the parties to try to work something out. The incentives for a defendant to bargain in exchange for a guilty plea are many, with the length of time to be spent in prison a dominant underlying factor. This widespread practice of plea bargaining where concessions are made by the prosecutor and the judge is the most typical way that justice is allocated. It is here that the needs and perspectives of system actors come into play.

"Plea bargaining" typically consists of an accommodation between the prosecutor and the defendant whereby a plea of guilty is exchanged for an agreement by the prosecutor to press a charge less serious than that warranted by the facts. It can also concern a recommendation for leniency by the prosecutor in his pre-sentence report to the judge. Most times, the defendant's objective is to be charged with a crime carrying a lower potential maximum sentence, thus limiting the discretion of the judge. A plea may also be entered on one charge upon agreement that the prosecutor will drop other charges in a multi-count indictment. Other reasons for seeking a lesser charge are to avoid legislatively mandated sentences or stipulations against probation, or to escape a charge which carries with it an undesirable label (rapist, homosexual). The prosecutor seeks to obtain a guilty plea so he can avoid combat in the courtroom. While the imposition of the sentence remains a function of the court, the prosecutor draws up the indictment.

According to the traditional conception, criminal cases are not "settled" as in civil law, but the outcome is determined through the symbolic combat of the state versus the accused. Yet as Newman found in Wisconsin, "Most of the convictions

(93.8%) were not convictions in a combative, trial by jury sense, but merely involved sentencing after a plea of guilty had been entered."[39] Although there is variation among jurisdictions, it has been estimated that 90 percent of all defendants charged with crimes before state and federal courts plead guilty rather than exercise their right to go to trial.[40] Table VI-1, developed by the President's Commission, shows the percentage of guilty pleas in several states and the United States District Courts. As noted, an average of 87 percent of those convicted in these districts chose to plead guilty.

Of further interest is the type of defendant who pleads guilty. Newman found that 84 percent of the recidivists immediately entered guilty pleas, while first offenders with counsel tended to change their plea to guilty after the initial charging procedures.[41] When a case does go to trial it is usually won by the prosecutor. Since he seeks to prevent a trial through compromise, there are incentives which demand that he take only those cases to court which he believes can be won.

The extent of plea bargaining is closely related to the degree of urbanization in a jurisdiction. There are, however, some cities

TABLE VI-1

GUILTY PLEA CONVICTIONS IN SEVERAL STATES
(1964 statistics unless otherwise indicated)

State	Total Convictions	Guilty Pleas	
		Number	Percentage
California (1965)	30,840	22,817	74.0
Connecticut	1,596	1,494	93.9
District of Columbia (year end June 30, 1964)	1,115	817	73.5
Hawaii	393	360	91.5
Illinois	5,591	4,768	85.2
Kansas	3,025	2,727	90.2
Massachusetts (1963)	7,790	6,642	85.2
Minnesota (1965)	1,567	1,437	91.7
New York	17,249	16,464	95.5
U.S. District Courts	29,170	26,273	90.2
Average			87.0

SOURCE: President's Commission on Law Enforcement and Administration of Justice, *Task Force Report: The Courts,* Washington, D.C., U.S. Government Printing Office, 1967, p. 9.

such as Philadelphia and Pittsburgh where less than one-third of the defendants use the "cop-out" route.[42] In these cities a system of expedited trials has reduced the administrative pressures for bargaining. There is probably a more realistic estimation by the police and prosecutor of the type of charge likely to be sympathetically received by the judge. The scanty available evidence seems to indicate that in rural areas there is greater variation in the level of guilty pleas. In such districts it might be suggested that personal relationships and custom exert a greater influence than the structural conditions imposed on the parties in urban situations.

Recorder's Court in Detroit has probably the most well-developed system of plea bargaining. Here, a "bargaining prosecutor" is always on duty to deal with the lawyers who line up for consultation. Close by his office is the pen where prisoners awaiting arraignment or trial are retained. The lawyers tread back and forth between the pen and the prosecutor's office negotiating the conditions under which each side will act when the case comes to open court.

The growth of bargain justice has been affected by such external factors as the volume of crime and the law explosion. At the same time, changes within the judicial system have increased administrative pressures while reducing some of the predictable elements in the process. The length of the average felony trial in the United States has increased so that the trial which took 1.9 days to complete in 1950, took 2.8 days to complete in 1965. Under the civil libertarian influence of the Supreme Court, a major share of judicial and prosecutorial resources have been diverted "from the trial of criminal cases to the resolution of pre-trial motions and post-conviction proceedings."[43]

The guilty plea has the manifest advantage of assisting in the processing of a large number of cases, but it also assures conviction of the guilty, all for a minimal expenditure of resources. From the organization's perspective, the guilty plea performs the latent function of helping to maintain the equilibrium and viability of the system. Not only does it help to achieve the efficient use of resources, but it also means that the system is able to operate in a more predictable environment. Because actors in the system do not have to expose themselves to the uncertainty of a jury trial, the cooperative—some might say symbiotic—relationships necessary for operation of the system are maintained.

From interviews with prisoners in New Jersey and Pennsylvania, Trebach found that an elaborate "plea inducing" machinery exists, which acts on the accused from the time that he is arrested until he is sentenced. The function of this machinery is to produce a high percentage of "cop-outs" —defendants who plead guilty in exchange for considerations. It is composed of a combination of "sound legal advice, intimidation, and mis-leading information"[44] which is directed at the accused by prosecutors, detectives, probation officers, family, and counsel. Intimidation becomes a factor when the prosecutor threatens to file multiple charges against the defendant or suggests that leniency will not be given in sentencing recommendations unless he "cops a plea."

The unpleasant surroundings in which the accused awaits trial may help to spur a guilty plea. By recommending that bail be either set high or denied, the prosecutor may hope to keep the defendant confined so that he can "think things over a little." Assisting in this process are conditions in short-term prisons (e.g., county jails), which the President's Commission found to be generally deplorable. More are overcrowded and lack recreational facilities; in contrast, the state penitentiary may look appealing. This environment is bound to assist the plea-inducement process. Prosecutors often counter such allegations with the statements that some attorneys prolong their client's stay in the pre-trial jail by obtaining continuances in an attempt to induce a plea or secure a more cooperative judge.

One of the risks inherent in bargain justice is that innocent defendants may plead guilty. Although it is hard to substantiate such cases, there is evidence that some defendants have entered guilty pleas when they had committed no criminal offense. Benjamin M. Davis, a San Francisco attorney represented a man charged with kidnapping and forcible rape. Although Davis was confident that the defendent was not guilty, the client elected to plead guilty to the lesser charge of simple battery. When Davis informed the accused that conviction on the charges seemed highly improbable, the reply was simply, "I can't take the chance."[45] Such cases often result either from confusion by the neophyte or because hardened criminals feel that they cannot risk a trial. When faced with the possibility that a jury may find him guilty of murder, an innocent defendant with a record may plead to the lesser charge of manslaughter.

Exchange Relationships in Plea Bargaining

The prosecutor and defense attorney each brings certain objectives to a bargaining session. Each has attempted to structure the situation to his own advantage and comes armed with a number of tactics designed to improve his position. Thus it is common for prosecutors to draw up multiple-offense indictments. As one defense attorney noted:

"Prosecutors throw everything into an indictment they can think of, down to and including spitting on the sidewalk. They then permit the defendant to plead guilt of one or two offenses, and he is supposed to think it's a victory."[46]

This is especially important to the prosecution when faced with a difficult case where, for instance, the complainant is reluctant, the value of the stolem item is questionable, and the reliability of the evidence is in doubt. Jackson reports that narcotics officers will often file sale charges against a defendant when they know they can convict only for possession. Since the accused knows that the penalty for selling is much greater, he will be tempted to plead to the lesser charge—of which he may or may not be guilty—rather than risk a jury trial which could send him to prison for a long time without a chance for parole.[47]

Defense counsel may approach these negotiations by threatening to ask for a jury trial if concessions are not made. His hand is further strengthened if he has filed pre-trial motions which require a formal response on the part of the prosecutor. Another tactic is to seek pre-trial continuances with the hope that witnesses will become unavailable, public interest will die, and memories of the incident will be shortened.

Since negotiations are worked out by the prosecutor and defense attorney, the interests of the public and even the defendant may become secondary to the needs of these principal actors. This becomes a severe problem when the defense attempts to bargain on a package basis, agreeing to trade the guilty pleas of some clients for promises of less severe treatment for others. Referring to a fellow lawyer, one Seattle respondent said:

> "You should see——. He goes up there to Carroll's office with a whole fist full of cases. He trades on some, bargains on others and never goes to court. It's amazing but it's the way he makes his living."

The bargaining session between counsel and prosecutor bears a striking resemblance to a formal ritual in which friendliness and joking mask the forceful presentation of antagonistic views. The pattern of each exchange is similar: initial humor, the advancing of each viewpoint, resolution of the conflict, and a final period spent cementing the relationship. Throughout the session each side tries to impress the other with the confidence he has in his own case, while indicating weaknesses in his opponent's presentation. All during the discussions there appears to be a norm of openness and candor directed toward maintenance of the relationship. Little effort seems to be made to conceal information which may be used by the adversary in the courtroom. Subin reports that there is a standing rule that "confidences shared during negotiations will not be used in court."[48] There are, of course, some attorneys who do not conform to this norm. A prosecutor told Alschuler:

> "There are some attorneys with whom we never bargain, because we can't. We don't like to penalize a defendant because he has an ass for an attorney, but when an attorney cannot be trusted, we have no alternative."[49]

In plea bargaining sessions, defense attorneys may not be equal competitors with the prosecution. They have limited investigative resources and are often unaware of the evidence held against their client. Under these circumstances it is necessary for defense attorneys to maintain good personal relationships with the prosecutor and his staff.

Through exchange, both the prosecutor and the defense attorney can assess the strength of the case against the accused. The resulting opinion will greatly affect the way in which the case is disposed. If the exchange reveals that the opponent has a stronger case than has been expected, a change in the bargaining tactics and demands is made.

Defense attorneys often feel that prosecutors are insulated from the human factors of a case and thus are unwilling to individualize justice. Since the defense lawyer gets to know the defendant, his problems, and his family, he becomes emotionally attached to the case.

> "We have to impress—— [the chief criminal deputy] with the fact that he is dealing with humans, not with just a case. If the guy is guilty he should be imprisoned, but he should get only what's coming to him, no more."

Of major concern to some defense lawyers is the threat that "habitual criminal laws" may be invoked against recidivist offenders. In some states the power to charge under this law, which carries with it an indeterminate sentence, can be used by the prosecutor as an ultimate weapon in plea bargaining. As a Seattle attorney approached a negotiation session, he opened with:

> "First, I hope that you're not going to 'bitch' this guy. I know that he has been a prior offender, but you're going to look sort of foolish trying to send him off on this sort of case."

A survey of the chief prosecution officials in various states by the University of Pennsylvania Law School revealed that the strength of the state's case was the most important (85%) motivation in their bargaining decision. The volume of the administrative workload (37%) and the harshness of the law (32%) were other important factors.[50]

Often the bargain is struck in ways which might go unnoticed by the casual observer. To maintain some distance between the adversaries, the author has noted that vague references are often made about the disposition of the case. Such statements as "I think I can sell this to the boss" or "I'll see what can be done" signal the completion of the session and are interpreted by the actors as an agreement on the terms of the exchange. On other cases, negotiations are more specific, with a direct promise made that certain charges will be altered in exchange for a guilty plea.

Neither partner in the exchange is a free agent since each depends upon the cooperation of the defendant and the judge. Attorneys often cite the difficulty which they have convincing a client that he should uphold his portion of the bargain. Newman reports that experienced criminals expressed the opinion that they are better off without a lawyer, since they can then deal directly with the prosecutor.[51] As Weintraub notes, "The cases are rare indeed in which the court rejects a plea upon which the District Attorney and the defendant have agreed."[52]

Sentencing

The maintenance of the bargaining system depends upon acceptance of the negotiated plea by the judge. It also requires that the judge fulfill the agreement by sentencing the accused according to the recommendation of the prosecutor. Because there are doubts about the legality and public acceptance of negotiated pleas, the judge and the defendant act out a little charade in which statements are elicited to show that the guilty plea is made without reservations, and without the promise of lenient treatment. Someone reading the court record would not be aware of the fact that the plea has been negotiated and that this verbal exchange consists of perjury which the judge knowingly ignores.

The negotiated plea is a fairly new concept in American criminal justice, one which we may not yet be ready to recognize fully. Thus, in *Shelton* v. *United States,* the Supreme Court did not face the question of the propriety of plea bargaining, but vacated the conviction after a confession of error by the Solicitor General. The court ruled that "the plea of guilty may have been improperly obtained," side-stepping the issue.[53] In general the courts have ruled that the plea must be understood and made voluntarily. In *Machibroda* v. *United States,* the Court said that "if the plea is induced by promises or threats which deprive it of its voluntary character, it is void."[54] In this way the courts have overruled pleas when it was apparent that the prosecutor made a "promise" as to what sentence the defendant was likely to get. Recent decisions by the Burger Court have continued this emphasis on the voluntary nature of the plea, but have also indicated a willingness to move toward the formal legitimation of the plea.[55]

The cooperation of the judge is crucial to a successful bargain. Although the judge's role prescription requires that he uphold the public interest, he may be reluctant to intervene and repudiate an agreement acceptable to the prosecutor and defendant. Thus it is common for both the prosecutor and defense attorney to confer with the judge regarding the sentence to be imposed. At the same time, the credibility of the myths surrounding the process requires that he hold in reserve his power to reject the agreement. Since uncertainty is one of the hazards of the administrative system, the judge's decisions will be used by observers as an indication of his future behavior.

Does the "cop-out" receive a lighter sentence than does the defendant who is found guilty through a trial? The evidence indicates that judges tend to consider a guilty plea a sign of repentance and believe that it denotes an interest by the defendant in his own rehabilitation. Judges responding to one questionnaire said that they tended to award less severe punishment following a guilty plea.[56] The paradox of this situation may mean that the defendant originally indicted for the more serious of two related crimes, but who pleads guilty, may receive less punishment than does the defendant indicted for a less serious offense, but found guilty through trial.

Justification

Public criticism of plea bargaining has erupted from time to time when defendants have been allowed to plead guilty to lesser charges stemming from widely publicized crimes. Laymen have often expressed displeasure when they discovered that symbolic combat was not the distinguishing feature of the judicial system. Others have been concerned with the "invisible" nature of the bargaining model. Most recently the guilty plea of James Earl Ray, given in connection with the assassination of Martin Luther King, Jr., caused a rash of editorials and other public manifestations of anger and confusion. Many of these critics felt that the acceptance of Ray's plea was unjustified, given the magnitude of the crime, while others expressed bewilderment that such procedures were followed. Negro groups suggested that a black man accused of the same crime would not have received such "lenient" treatment.

As late as the 1920's the legal profession was united in opposition to plea bargaining. Roscoe Pound, Raymond Moley, and others associated with the crime surveys of the period stressed the opportunities for political influence as a factor in the administration of criminal justice. Today, under the pressures generated by crime in an urban society and the reality of bargaining, a shift has occurred so that professional groups are primarily interested in procedures which will allow for the review of guilty pleas and other safeguards. Thus the American Bar Association has proposed minimum standards for the acceptance of guilty pleas.[57] The President's Commission has acknowledged that

> "Plea bargaining may be a useful procedure especially in congested urban jurisdictions, but neither the dignity of the law, nor the quality of justice, nor the protection of society from dangerous criminals is enhanced by its becoming conducted covertly."[58]

With few exceptions, the current emphasis of legal scholars is to erect standards designed to eliminate abuses in plea bargaining, while maintaining the procedure as an open, legitimate aspect of the justice system.

One of the most commonly asserted justifications for plea bargaining is that it is necessary to individualize justice. Traditionally judges have performed this function. It can be argued, however, that developments in the system have limited the discretion of the judge, while increasing the opportunity for the prosecutor to allocate justice. Because of this factor, it is suggested that if the criminal law is to be even minimally fair, the prosecutor's office must become a ministry of justice, able to administratively determine case outcomes. Although questions of fact should be answered by a judge and jury, criminal justice often involves such intangible issues as entrapment, intent, and self-defense, which might be more equitably resolved through the pre-courtroom discussions of the prosecutor and defense attorney. Even such critics as Alschuler have admitted that plea bargaining "has a marked advantage over traditional forms of adjudication in that it is a more flexible method of administering justice." But, as he further notes, "the utility of discretion must be balanced against the utility of pre-ordained rules, which can limit the importance of subjective judgments, promote equality, control corruption, and provide a basis for planning, both before and after controversies arise."[59]

A major factor promoting the guilty plea is related to the nature of statutory law and the activities of legislatures which have dictated mandatory sentences for certain crimes. In their haste to appease the public, legislatures have often fixed penalties which are inconsistent with the aggravated level of the crime. For example, the Nixon Administration's attempt to change the laws concerning possession and use of marijuana was based in large part on the fact that the penalties required by the law were not consistent with the crime. As a felony, possession by a young, first offender could result in a prison sentence longer than that imposed for such "greater" crimes as rape and robbery. As one defense attorney has said, "Our sentencing laws are exceedingly severe and if they were strictly applied, they would be great breeders of disrespect for the law."[60] By accepting a guilty plea to a lesser offense, the prosecutor and judge may help to mitigate the harshness of the letter of the law.

An axiom of our legal tradition maintains that a judge should retain sentencing discretion so that he can fit the punishment to the individual. When the legislature has preempted the judicial power by requiring that a mandatory nonsuspendable sentence be imposed, the only way which the defendant's counsel can help his guilty client secure justice is to negotiate for a lesser charge. Under such circumstances the defendant may have to give up the chance that although guilty of the more serious crime, his unblemished record would insure that he be given a light sentence. Newman found that in Michigan and Kansas, where the legislatures have restricted judicial discretion, bargaining was more prominent than in Wisconsin, where the judge has considerably more freedom.[61]

A second justification for plea bargaining is that of administrative necessity. As we have seen, the problem of criminal justice is that of mass production. In our increasingly complex society the demands on the judicial process are overwhelming. Calendar congestion, the size of the prison population, and strains on judicial personnel have been cited as shortcomings in the system. One Los Angeles trial judge caught the essence of the matter when he told an investigator, "We are running a machine. We know we have to grind them out fast." A Manhattan prosecutor has said, "Our office keeps eight courtrooms extremely busy trying five percent of the cases. If even ten percent of the cases ended in a trial, the system would break down. We can't afford to think very much about anything else."[63] Yet, as Rosett notes, there are courts in large urban areas where guilty pleas are not used.[64]

Criticism of plea bargaining is generally based on the fact that it is hidden from judicial scrutiny. Because the agreement is most often made at an early stage of the proceedings, the judge has little information about the crime or the defendant and is not able to review prosecutorial judgment. As a result, there is no judicial review of the propriety of the bargain—no check on the amount of pressure applied to the defendant so that he pleads guilty. Unconstitutional behavior may contribute to successful prosecution. The police may engage in illegal searches, neglect the procedural rights of the defendant, and engage in "stationhouse punishment" because they know that the case will never come to trial. Exclusionary rules designed to discourage illegal conduct are ineffective in this situation. As the President's Commission rightly notes, "The results of bargain justice is that the judge, the public, and sometimes even the defendant cannot know for certain who got what, from whom, in exchange for what."[65]

JURY

Only about 8 percent of criminal cases are disposed of through jury trial, yet "the benefits of trial by jury" is one of the most ingrained features of the American ideology; it is mentioned in the Declaration of Independence, three amendments to the Constitution, and countless opinions of the Supreme Court. Although the jury trial accounts for only a small fraction of prosecutions, it has a decided impact on the decisions made in the criminal justice process. We have noted the influence of the potential call for a jury trial on decisions to prosecute, negotiations for a guilty plea, and sentencing behavior of the judges. Klaven and Zeisel, the authors of the monumental study, *The American Jury,* have said:

"Thus the jury is not controlling merely the immediate case before it, but the host of cases not before it which are destined to be disposed of by the pre-trial process. The jury thus controls not only the formal resolution of controversies in the criminal case, but also the informal resolution of cases that never reach the trial stage. In a sense the jury, like the visible cap of an iceberg, exposes but a fraction of its true volume."[66]

The use of juries varies throughout the United States, and within the framework of state law the choice of jury or bench trial is generally left open to the defendant. This decision is influenced primarily by the nature of the crime, community norms, and the past record of the trial judge. Juries are waived in only about 30 percent of murder prosecutions, but in 90 percent of forgeries. Defendants in Wisconsin waive the right to a jury trial in approximately 75 percent of criminal cases, while in Utah only 5 percent prefer bench trials.[67] In addition, it seems to be widely assumed that because of court congestion judges normally penalize defendants who do not waive their right to a jury trial. Available evidence points to the fact that defense counsel generally have a very accurate estimate of the relative leniency of the judge or jury.[68]

Jury Selection

The problem of selecting a fair and impartial jury received widespread publicity during the trials of Black Panthers Huey P. Newton and Bobby Seale. A persistent criticism voiced by black militants is that they cannot receive a fair trial because American juries are not composed of their "peers" but of middle-class whites with racist attitudes who are predisposed to find them guilty.[69] It can be easily demonstrated that jury selection methods discriminate against the lower-occupational groups, excluding them from being considered for jury duty. Not only does this create juries which are unrepresentative of the community, but the class bias influences decision-making within the jury room. Studies have shown that regardless of the supposed equality of the jury members, higher-status males tend to dominate the deliberations and are most prone to finding defendants guilty.[70]

Theoretically every member of the community should have an equal chance of being chosen for jury duty; however, the methods of selection are quite specific in stipulating various qualifications which exclude citizens with certain characteristics. In most states jurors must be registered voters. In addition, certain occupational categories such as doctors, lawyers, teachers, and policemen are excluded, since their services are needed or because of their connection with the court. In many localities it is possible to be excused if service will present economic or physical hardship.

The methods used to draw up the jury list of "pool" further skews the selection process.[71] The most common method is through the "key-man" system in which names of prospective jurors are submitted by "sponsors" such as judges, postmasters, service organizations, or party committeemen. Given the well-known fact that individuals socialize with members of their own class with shared opinions, the cultural bias is evident.

A second method uses public lists such as voter registration rosters, tax records, and telephone directories to obtain names for the pool. In Alameda County, California, for example, the county-wide voter registration is 82 percent of all eligible persons, yet in the predominately lower-class black area of West Oakland only 52.5 percent were registered. In addition, subjective standards such as "good character," "approved judgment," and "integrity" give the jury commissioners more leeway in determining who is to be placed in the pool. In Alameda County a test is used to determine intelligence; the failure rate among white suburban community residents was 14.5 percent, whereas 81.5 percent of the black lower class failed.[72]

All of these criteria have an obvious effect upon the jury pools which are created. In one of the few comparative studies John Vanderzell found that in Lancaster County, Pennsylvania, which employs a key-man system, males, retired persons, and the managerial class were overrepresented; in Philadelphia County, which uses voter registration lists, females, clerical workers, and whites were overrepresented; in Allegheny County, which uses tax lists, the managerial and professional classes were overrepresented.[73] Through narrowing the sources of potential jurors, the inherent cultural bias has been institutionalized by the administrative system.

By examining over 3,500 criminal trials in which juries played a part, Kalven and Zeisel attempted to isolate those factors which influenced the decision-making process.[74] As shown in Table VI-2, the judge and jury agreed in 75.4 percent of the trials. Also of interest is the very high rate of conviction; supporting the idea that the filtering process has removed the doubtful cases before trial. The table also shows that a jury is evidently more lenient than a judge. The total conviction rate by juries is 64.3 percent, while judges voted for conviction in 83.3 percent of the cases. Presumably because the judge has more experience with the process, he is more prone to confer the guilty label on defendants who survive the examination of the police and prosecutor.

The value of the jury system has long been debated. Jerome

TABLE VI-2
VERDICT OF JURY AND JUDGE

		Jury		
		Acquits	Convicts	Hangs
Judge	Acquits	13.4	2.2	1.1
	Convicts	16.9	.7[a] 56.8 4.5[b]	4.4

SOURCE: Harry Kalven and Hans Zeisel, *The American Jury* (Chicago: University of Chicago Press, 1966), pp. 56, 60. Table constructed from Table 11, p. 56, and Table 13, p. 60.
a. Jury convicts on major count, judge on lesser.
b. Jury convicts on lesser count, judge on major.

Frank noted in the 1930's that "jury-made law" was the best example of that which is capricious and arbitrary.[75] From time to time public interest has been aroused by this controversy, yet criticism seems to ebb and flow depending upon the values of the observers. Thus liberals were quite upset that the jury did not make a "clear decision" in the case of the "Chicago Seven," yet hailed the importance of the jury system and the decision in the New Haven trial of certain Black Panthers. What must be kept in mind is that juries are a factor in only a small number of the criminal decisions made in this country. Our political myths may have obscured this fact.

JUDICIAL DECISION-MAKING

The final step in the criminal justice process is the passing of sentences upon the guilty. Statutes usually allow the judge discretion as to the punishment which he may give, although sometimes legislatures have been quite specific in designating madatory sentences for some violations. The judge's discretion is also limited by the exchange relations which he has with the other actors in the process. He must secure their cooperation to make his own job easier. Although legal values stress the need to individualize justice, this may be viewed as the "sentencing burden" from the judge's perspective, since there may be no logical coherence among the facts of the case, the statutory scale of punishments, and the characteristics of the convicted. Some jurists may ease this burden by routinizing the process, making punishments fit categories of crimes without paying attention to the attributes of the offender.

Individual differences in the sentencing tendencies of judges have fascinated social scientists. Research done over fifty years ago in New York City showed that the forty-one magistrates varied from the most lenient, who discharged 74 percent of the accused brought before him, to the most severe, who let only 7 percent go.[75] More recently, a study of Chicago's Women's Court revealed that the proportion of shoplifting cases found not guilty ranged from 5 percent to 20 percent, and the number of probations from 10 to 62 percent.[76] Green found that the degree of disparity among judges in Philadelphia was most pronounced in those cases at the intermediate level of gravity, tapering off gradually as the cases approached the polarities of mildness or seriousness. When the offense was serious there was a high degree of consistency among judges in the length of penitentiary sentences which they imposed.[77]

That judges exhibit different sentencing proclivities is taken as a fact of life by criminal lawyers and more recidivists. As early as 1933, Gaudet, Harris, and St. John reported that

"some recidivists know the sentencing tendencies of judges so well that the accused will frequently attempt to choose which is to sentence them, and further, some lawyers say they are frequently able to do this."[78]

In those court systems where the assignment of judges is decentralized, both the prosecution and defense may engage in a sparring contest to move a case to a judge whose attitudes are consistent with theirs. In centralized systems where cases are assigned to judges on a rotational basis, influence with the clerk or use of continuances are often used to shift cases.

These disparities among judges may be ascribed to a number of factors: the conflicting goals of criminal justice, the fact that judges are a product of different backgrounds, and the influence of the community within the political context of the system.

Each of these factors to some extent structures the judge's exercise of discretion. In addition, it can be suggested that a judge's perception of these factors is dependent to some degree on his own attitudes toward the law, a particular crime, or a particular offender.

Even though sentencing is the responsibility of the judge, other persons may participate in the decision-making process. In many states the pre-sentence report has become an important ingredient in the judicial mix. Usually a probation officer investigates the convicted person's background, criminal record, job status, and mental condition to suggest a resolution of the case which is in the interests of both the individual and of society. The probation officer may, of necessity, use hearsay as well as firsthand information. There is no opportunity for the defendant to challenge the contents of the report or the probation department's recommendation.

The pre-sentence report is one way the judge eases the strain of decision-making, shifting his responsibility to the probation department. Since there are a substantial number of sentencing alternatives open to the judge, he may rely upon the report for guidance. Carter and Wilkins conclude, after studying sentencing decisions in California, that there is a high correlation between the probation recommendation and the court's disposition of individual cases.[79] The pre-sentence report and the activity of the probation department adds to the mythology of the criminal court as a treatment center. From an organizational standpoint the probation department is supposed to be independent of other parts of the judicial system, yet from the standpoint of the politics of administration, it, too, is tied to the court structure. Rather than presenting an independent and impartial report, probation officers may be more interested in second-guessing the judge.

Who receives unfavorable treatment as a result of a sentencing decision? Our initial impression would lead us to suspect that out-groups would receive the longest prison terms, the highest fines, and be placed on probation the fewest times. Although some investigations have sustained these assumptions, the evidence is not totally conclusive.

Bullock found that blacks received harsher sentences than whites for some offenses, but lighter than whites for others. To some extent this reflects the indulgent and nonindulgent patterns that characterize racial attitudes concerning property and intergroup morals. To a great extent local and regional attitudes play an important role. As Bullock concludes, "Those who enforce the law conform to the norms of the local society concerning racial prejudice, thus denying equality before the law."[80] However, Green found that no racial differences in sentencing practices could be found in his study of 1,400 cases handled without jury in the Philadelphia Court of Quarter Sessions, especially when prior record was taken into account.[81] Atkinson and Neuman found that judges exercised sentencing discretion in favor of younger persons, women, hometowners, and those employed.[82]

Although political scientists have been interested in the decisions of members of the United States Supreme Court, there have been very few examinations of the sentencing behavior by judges in criminal courts. The study by Green, referred to above, is probably the major work in this area.[83] Rather than determining sentences on a whim he found that judges are influenced to a large extent by the facts of the case such as the degree of specificity of the victim and the amount of direct contact between offender and victim. In addition, the extent to which the criminal act involves bodily injury has bearing. Beside these factors which emphasize the seriousness of the crime, differences in social background, personality, and penal philosophy are seen as making individual judges react differently to cases of equivalent gravity. Our knowledge of judicial decision-making is still at the primitive stage of scholarly development.

Like other actors in the judicial process, the judge plays his role within the context of a political and administrative system. Although he is expected to subscribe to the due process values, he finds himself in an organization where his influence and ability to perform his tasks are affected by his relationships with the prosecutor, defense attorneys, and actors outside the judicial system. Bargain justice operates so that most cases are resolved through administrative decisions before the defendant appears in the courtroom. In those few cases which come to trial, the stakes for all of the participants become more visible and the exchange relationships more involved. In many ways cases disposed of through trial contain the threat of a greater potential loss to all actors. To a great extent it would seem that the jury trial has become a tribunal of last resort when the administrative or political facts do not allow a negotiated solution to a case.

NOTES

1. Jerome Frank, *Courts on Trial* (New York: Atheneum, 1963), 4.

2. U.S., President's Commission on Law Enforcement and Administration of Justice, *The Challenge of Crime in a Free Society*, 1967, 128.

3. Milton D. Green, "The Business of the Trial Courts," *The Courts, The Public and the Law Explosion*, Harry W. Jones (ed.) (Englewood Cliffs: Prentice Hall, 1965), 13.

4. Jerome Skolnick, "Social Control in the Adversary System," Journal of Conflict Resolution, 11 (March, 1967), 56.

5. Alexander B. Smith and Abraham S. Blumberg, "The Problem of Objectivity in Judicial Decision-Making," Social Forces, 46 (September, 1967), 96.

6. Ibid., 99.

7. Abraham S. Blumberg, *Criminal Justice* (Chicago: Quadrangle, 1967), 118.

8. Michael Lipsky, "Toward a Theory of Street-Level Bureaucracy," paper presented at the Annual Meeting of the American Political Science Association, 1969.

9. Caleb Foote, "Vagrancy-type Law and Its Administration," University of Pennsylvania Law Review, 104 (1965), 603-650.

10. "Metropolitan Criminal Courts of First Instance," Harvard Law Review, 70 (1956), 320.

11. Stephen R. Bing and S. Stephen Rosenfeld, *The Quality of Justice in the Lower Criminal Courts of Metropolitan Boston*, Report of the Lawyers Committee for Civil Rights Under Law, 1970.

12. President's Commission, *Task Force Report: The Courts*, 66.

13. Ibid.

14. Richard A. Watson and Rondal G. Downing, *The Politics of the Bench and the Bar: Judicial Selection Under the Missouri Non-Partisan Court Plan* (New York: John Wiley, 1969), 254.

15. Editorial, *Journal of the American Judicature* (1964), 124.

16. Wallace S. Sayre and Herbert Kaufman, *Governing New York City* (New York: Norton, 1965), 538.

17. Ibid., 542.

18. Edward N. Costikyan, *Behind Closed Doors* (New York: Harcourt Brace &

World, 1966), 176. But see: Martin and Susan Tolchin, *To the Victor . . . Political Patronage from the Clubhouse to the White House* (New York: Random House, 1971).

19. Herbert Mitgang, *The Man Who Rode the Tiger: The Life and Times of Judge Samuel Seabury* (Philadelphia: Lippincott, 1963).

20. Watson and Downing, 42.

21. See: John E. Crow, "Subterranean Politics: A Judge Is Chosen," Journal of Public Law, 12 (1963), 275.

22. For example: Edward Banfield and James Q. Wilson, *City Politics* (Cambridge: Harvard University Press and the M.I.T. Press, 1963).

23. Herbert Jacob, "The Effect of Institutional Differences in the Recruitment Process: The Case of State Judges," Journal of Public Law, 13 (1964), 107.

24. Stuart Nagel, *The Legal Process from a Behavioral Perspective* (Homewood, Ill.: Dorsey Press, 1969), 227.

25. Martin A. Levin, "An Empirical Evaluation of Urban Political Systems: The Criminal Courts," paper presented at the Annual Meeting of the American Political Science Association, 1969.

26. Ibid., 3.

27. Ibid., 10.

28. President's Commission, *Task Force Report: The Courts*, 32.

29. Blumberg, 47.

30. Smith and Blumberg, 97-98.

31. Ibid.

32. David Sudnow, "Normal Crimes: Sociological Features of the Penal Code in a Public Defender Office," Social Problems, 12 (Winter, 1965), 255-276.

33. Blumberg, 39.

34. Frederic Suffet, "Bail Setting: A Study of Courtroom Interaction," Crime and Delinquency, 12 (October, 1966), 318-331.

35. Ibid., 330.

36. Laura Banfield and C. David Anderson, "Continuances in the Cook County Criminal Courts," University of Chicago Law Review, 35 (1968), 259.

37. Blumberg, 78-88.

38. Robert Polstein, "How to 'Settle' a Criminal Case: The Art of Negotiating Lesser Pleas and Sentences," *The Problem of a Criminal Defense* (Chicago: American Law Institute, 1961).

39. Donald J. Newman, A Study of Informal Processes in Felony Convictions" (Unpublished Ph.D. Dissertation, University of Wisconsin, 1954).

40. See: *Law Enforcement in the Metropolis*, Donald M. McIntyre, Jr., ed. (Chicago: American Bar Foundation, 1967), 132; Donald J. Newman, *Conviction: The Determination of Guilt or Innocence without Trial* (Chicago: American Bar Foundation, 1966); Dominick R. Vetri, "Plea Bargaining: Compromises by Prosecutors to Secure Guilty Pleas," University of Pennsylvania Law Review, 112 (April, 1964), 865-908.

41. Donald J. Newman, "Pleading Guilty for Considerations: A Study of Bargain Justice," Journal of Criminal Law, Criminology and Police Science, 46 (March-April, 1956), 780-790.

42. Albert W. Alschuler, "The Prosecutor's Role in Plea Bargaining," University of Chicago Law Review, 36 (Fall, 1968), 61. See also: Martin A. Levin, "Urban Political Systems and Judicial Behavior: The Criminal Courts in Minneapolis and Pittsburgh" (Unpublished Ph.D. Dissertation, Harvard University, 1970), iv-9.

43. Alschuler, 50.

44. Arnold Trebach, *The Rationing of Justice* (New Brunswick: Rutgers University Press, 1964), 85.

45. Alschuler, 61.

46. Ibid., 86.

47. Bruce Jackson, *A Thief's Primer* (New York: Macmillan, 1969), 132.

48. Harry I. Subin, *Criminal Justice in a Metropolitan Court* (Washington: Office of Criminal Justice, United States Department of Justice, 1966), 47. Also: Comment, "Official Inducements to Plead Guilty: Suggested Morals for a Marketplace," University of Chicago Law Review, 32 (Autumn, 1964), 164-187.

49. Alschuler, 87.

50. Vetri, 901.

51. Newman, "Pleading Guilty," 783.

52. Ruth Weintraub and Rosalind Tough, "Lesser Pleas Considered," Journal of Criminal Law and Criminology, 32 (1942), 506.

53. *Shelton* v. *United States,* 356 U.S. 26 (1958).

54. *Machibroda* v. *United States,* 368 U.S. 487 (1962).

55. *United States* v. *Wallace,* 217 F. Supp. 518 (1963), *Parker* v. *North Carolina,* 397 U.S. 790 (1970), *North Carolina* v. *Alford,* 400 U.S. 25 (1970).

56. "The Influence of the Defendant's Plea on Judicial Determination of Sentencing," Yale Law Journal, 66 (1956), 204-220. Also: Newman, "Pleading Guilty"; Treback, esp. Ch. 9.

57. *American Bar Association Project on Minimum Standards for Criminal Justice, Standards Relating to Pleas of Guilty* (Tent. Draft, 1967).

58. President's Commission, *The Challenge of Crime in a Free Society,* 11.

59. Alschuler, 71.

60. Harry B. Steinberg, "A Conversation with Defense Counsel on the Problems of a Criminal Defense," *The Problem of a Criminal Defense,* 10.

61. Newman, *Conviction,* 53-56, 177-184.

62. Alschuler, 54.

63. Ibid., 55.

64. Arthur Rosett, "The Negotiated Guilty Plea," Annals, 374 (1967), 73.

65. President's Commission, *Task Force Report: The Courts,* 9-10.

66. Harry Kalven and Hans Zeisel, *The American Jury* (Chicago: University of Chicago Press, 1966), 31-32.

67. Ibid., 26-32.

68. Dallin H. Oaks and Warren Lehman, *A Criminal Justice System and the Indigent* (Chicago: University of Chicago Press, 1968), 53-57.

69. Jennie Rhine, "The Jury: A Reflection of the Prejudices of the Community," Hastings Law Journal, 20 (1969), 1417.

70. Fred L. Strodtbeck, Rita M. James, and Charles Hawkins, "Social Status in Jury Deliberations," American Sociological Review, 22 (December, 1957), 713-719.

71. Charles A. Linquist, "An Analysis of Juror Selection Procedure in the United States District Courts," Temple Law Quarterly, 41 (1967), 32-50.

72. Rhine, 1424.

73. John H. Vanderzell, "The Jury As a Community Cross-Section," Western Political Quarterly, 19 (1966), 136-149.

74. Kalven and Zeisel, 62.

75. Jerome Frank, *Courts on Trial* (New York: Atheneum, 1949), 132.

76. Harry W. Jones, "The Trial Judge—Role Analysis and Profile," *The Courts, The Public and the Law,* Harry W. Jones (ed.) (Englewood Cliffs: Prentice Hall, 1965), 140.

77. Mary Owen Cameron, *The Booster and the Snitch* (New York: Free Press, 1964).

78. Edward Green, *Judicial Attitudes in Sentencing* (London: Macmillan, 1961).

79. Frederick J. Gaudet, G. S. Harris, and C. W. St. John, "Individual Differences in the Sentencing Tendencies of Judges," Journal of Criminal Law and Criminology, 23 (January-February, 1933), 814. Also: Wayne Morse and Ronald H. Beattie, "A Study of the Variances in Sentences Imposed by Circuit Judges," *Oregon Law Review,* 11 (June, 1962).

80. Robert M. Carter and Leslie T. Wilkins, "Some Factors in Sentencing Policy," Journal of Criminal Law, Criminology, and Police Science, 58 (December, 1967), 503-514.

81. Henry Allen Bullock, "Significance of the Racial Factor in the Length of Prison Sentence," Journal of Criminal Law, Criminology and Police Science, 52 (November-December, 1961), 411-417.

82. Green, 98-99.

83. David N. Atkinson and Dale A. Neuman, "Judicial Attitudes and Defendant Attributes: Some Consequences for Municipal Court Decision-Making," Journal of Public Law, 19 (1970), 69-88.

84. See also: Nagel, 227.

DUE PROCESS IN AN

ADMINISTRATIVE SYSTEM

"Justice will be universal in this country when the processes as well as the doors of the courthouse are open to everyone."[1]

The Warren Court will be remembered for its attempt to insist that constitutional guarantees be extended throughout the administration of criminal justice. Long concerned with the rights of individuals in the courtroom, the justices of the Supreme Court directed their attention during the 1960's to pre-trial rights with a series of decisions which have the intention of bolstering adversary elements in the system.[2] The rationale for this shift is well stated by Justice Goldberg for the Court in *Escobedo* vs. *Illinois,* when quoting from Justice Black's dissent in the case of *In Re Groban* he notes that

"the right to use counsel at the formal trial [would be] a very hollow thing [if], for all practical purposes the conviction is already assured by pre-trial examination."[3]

By requiring that, among other rights, counsel be provided from the time that the accused arrives in the stationhouse, the Court has shown its concern about the inequalities which exist during the early stages of the administration of justice.

That there should be no mistake about the Court's intention, the chief justice set forth standards in *Miranda* vs. *Arizona* which have to be followed from the time a suspect enters the judicial process.[4] These mandates are that notice be given to a person that he has the right to remain silent, that statements he makes may be used as evidence against him, and that he has a right to the presence of an attorney, either appointed or retained. In effect the Warren Court has said that it is not enough for the states to follow procedures which allow for "fundamental fairness"; there must be absolute compliance by state and local officials with the provisions of the Bill of Rights.

Behind the Court's legal scholarship stands a desire to increase adversary elements in the process so that inequalities resulting from the social and economic status of defendants will be reduced. The Court put further emphasis behind these goals by easing accessibility of state prisoners to habeas corpus pleas in the federal district courts. By a narrow margin the Court split 5-4 in *Townsend* vs. *Sain* on this question, leaving many judges and lawyers aghast at the vast number of jailhouse petitions which followed.[5] Justice Burger noted in his "State of the Federal Judiciary" message this increase from eighty-nine in 1940 to twelve thousand in 1970.[6] Congress had made an effort through legislation to shut off this flow.

Until 1961, when it ruled that states could not use evidence obtained in violation of the Fourth Amendment's restrictions on unreasonable searches and seizures, the Supreme Court had insisted that states maintain only standards of "fundamental fairness" in the criminal justice process.[7] This meant that only the most blatant examples of injustice in criminal administration were outlawed by the Court. Thus the 1923 murder convictions of five Negroes sentenced to death after a forty-five-minute trial dominated by a mob were overturned, as was a confession beaten out of two Mississippi defendants by deputies using metal-studded belts. As Justice Cardozo noted, the test for determining the legitimacy of state action was to ask if the due process of law had been denied to a citizen by practices which violated those "fundamental principles of justice which lie at the base of our civil and political institutions." From the 1920's until the "due process revolution" of the 1960's the Court adhered to this principle, only gradually incorporating the rights of citizens from state actions to come under the protection of the Bill of Rights.

The political reaction to the decisions of the Warren Court were immediate and vociferous, especially when they concerned restrictions on police activities. Senator Sam Ervin, with the endorsement of fifteen colleagues, proposed a constitutional amendment designed to overrule *Miranda*. The McClellan Subcommittee held hearings on a variety of proposals to restrict the Court's decisions. Many of these congressional efforts resulted in the Omnibus Crime Control Act of 1968, which contained provisions designed to circumvent the Court. Congressional debate of the proposals was based, in part, on the notion that there was a direct causal relationship between the actions of the justices and the amount of crime. As part of Richard Nixon's 1968 presidential campaign, the liberals on the Court and Attorney General Ramsey Clark came under fire; the candidate promised that he would appoint "strict constructionists" to the high bench to reverse the due process trend.[9]

The charges that the Supreme Court was "coddling criminals" hit the public at a time when crime rates were on the rise and many American cities were feeling the effects of riots by blacks. In 1965 a Gallup Poll showed that 48 percent of the public believed that the courts were too lenient with criminal defendants; by 1968 63 percent so felt. Graham's analysis shows that unfortunately for the Court, good intentions were betrayed by violent times.[10]

With the retirement of Earl Warren, the Burger Court has continued to receive appeals challenging practices by criminal justice officials at the state and local level. Although the Warren Court left few criminal issues for others to decide the Court reconstituted by Richard Nixon is facing questions concerning plea bargaining, the role of grand juries, and capital punishment. If the first year's work by the new court is an indication of what is to follow, we can expect little backtracking to the conditions of the pre-Warren era; rather, as Graham suggests, there will probably be an interregnum in the effort to bring police practices under the Constitution.[11] Public interest in this area of the Court's activity seems to have lessened. In addition neither the use of the exclusionary rule nor the practices required by *Miranda* seem to have greatly hampered law enforcement officials in spite of their rhetoric.

Throughout this book it has been argued that criminal justice is allocated through an administrative system in which informal relationships and the survival needs of the organization become more important than the rights of the accused. Too often this means that the poor receive a very different brand of justice than do those who can afford counsel, who have influence, and whose cultural values are consistent with those of the dominant society. The rich are able to exaggerate the contentious procedure of the adversary system so that trials are either delayed or extended, the rules of evidence are precisely enforced, and the state must exert a supreme effort to secure conviction. This often means that the well-placed are not found guilty of crimes which it is reasonable to suspect that they have committed. Further, such trials delay the processing of other cases, overtax prosecution efforts, and demean the process by presenting the fact that with money it is possible to beat the system through "technicalities." Criminal justice in the United States today is an example of contrasts—many people are processed without the full benefit of constitutional rights, while others are able to defeat the demands of justice.

Reform advocates, including the President's Commission on Law Enforcement and Administration of Justice, have urged additional court facilities, better policemen, and more judges to solve the problems of the criminal justice system. In a 1970 address to the American Bar Association, Chief Justice Burger placed great stress upon creating the profession of court administrator to increase the efficiency of the process.[12] These suggestions place too much emphasis on the assumption that a reduction in case backlog and the replacement of certain types of administrators will correct the discrepancies of the process. Such a view reflects a misunderstanding of the organizational relationships within the judicial bureaucracy and the political impact of the community on the system. As one scholar has suggested:

"So long as law-enforcement agencies are subject to the will and desires of middle- and upper-class members of the community but are free to behave as they wish without fear or reprisal toward lower-class members of the community, then the legal system will continue to function in the highly discriminatory way that it now does."[13]

The contact of upper-middle-class youth with the police and the criminal justice process as a result of the anti-Vietnam demonstrations and the drug culture may be a force for change in the system. These young people and their parents are being exposed to conditions and treatment which the poor have always known.

Increased urbanization in a technically complex society has placed a greater burden on the judicial process, something predicted by Pound over forty years ago. He observed in 1930:

"Institutions and doctrines and precepts devised or shaped for rural and small-town conditions are failing to function efficiently under metropolitan conditions. . . ."[14]

To cope with the pressures caused by an expanded caseload, the maintenance needs of enforcement agencies, and a public concerned about the growth of violent crime, the legal system has placed greater emphasis upon administrative decision-making in the pre-trial period. As shown by the data which we have presented, the primary objective of law officials is to screen out those cases which do not contain the elements necessary for a speedy prosecution and conviction. For most of the actors engaged in judicial dcisions, their interests are enhanced if the adversary emphasis of the due process model is softened through bargaining among the participants. Describing the system which operates in New York County, Mayer summarizes the situation in most metropolitan areas:

"What we really have here is an administrative system of criminal justice, where the evidence is weighed and the important decisions are taken in the prosecutor's office."[15]

The Supreme Court has reacted to bargain justice by attempting to move the essence of the adversary system back into the earlier administrative stages of the criminal process.

The attention given the Warren Court's "due process revolution" is a measure of our belief in the "upper-court myth" and the efficacy of its decisions. Students of judicial politics have pointed out that in many arenas the decisions read by the justices in Washington have little bearing on the local officials charged with implementing them.[16] As Levine and Becker note, "The Supreme Court, like other political institutions, can allocate both material and symbolic values."[17] Decisions about material values result in direct and immediate alterations in the behavior of people and institutions. "The Court acts symbolically when it supports or denounces certain values and interests *without itself* substantially changing ongoing ways of life."[18] This means that as a result of the structure of the judiciary and the nature of the political process, the Supreme Court is unable to bring about behavioral changes in many societal arenas. Criminal justice would appear to be such a symbolic arena.

Although the Supreme Court may issue decisions, it is in the local courts and police stations where the opinions are implemented. Investigations of the impact of the criminal justice decisions generally show that the police have not been handcuffed, as had been proclaimed, and that for most defendants the prescribed warnings have had little effect. In New Haven, law students observing the police during the summer of 1966 found that even with the presence of observers detectives gave all of the *Miranda* advice in only 25 of 118 cases.[19] In Washington, researchers from Georgetown University Law School found that even though the police warned suspects about their rights, only a few requested counsel even though it was available around the clock. Those arrested continued to submit to interrogation even when they knew a lawyer was coming.[20] In Pittsburgh it was found that although confessions declined by 16 percent following *Miranda,* the conviction rate remained stable at about 67 percent, and the percentage of cases "cleared" actually rose slightly in the years following the decision. Although this would seem to show that the decision was having its desired effect, the Pittsburgh investigators reported that there had been an increased number of cases where indictments had not been brought. The impact of *Miranda* has probably been to make the police somewhat more cautious.[21]

These studies show that the impact of *Miranda* on the administration of criminal justice has not been great. Defendants either do not understand the warnings or have such a low feeling of efficacy that they are unable to exercise their rights. The police may imply that suspects who request a lawyer or who refuse to cooperate will be dealt with severely. There is also the fact that the police stations are fairly secure from the prying eyes of civil libertarians. There is no way of knowing how the warnings are being administered.

The exclusionary rule, the technique used by the Supreme Court to enforce due process criteria, also demonstrates the weakness of attempts to prescribe police conduct. Questioning suspects in ways which violate *Miranda* is useful to the police even though the evidence obtained may be later excluded. Not only do such practices lead to other information which is admissible, but the police and prosecutors may be more interested in their "clearance rate" than in securing convictions. The norms of secrecy, loyalty, and authority which infuse the police culture strengthen resistance to the changes prescribed by the judiciary.

If the effect of the Supreme Court's decisions in this arena are primarily symbolic, what does this mean for the administration of criminal justice? Levine and Becker suggest that the major impact of the Court "is to expand the scope of political conflict and to confer legitimacy on particular adversaries who are competing for political gains."[22] The mechanistic procedures outlined by the Court have not changed the rituals of police investigations, but the resulting furor has publicized deficiencies in the judicial system and has goaded "other political actors—legislators, Presidents, voters—to take sides in the conflict."[23] Public discussion of the rise in crime and the charges that the Court is coddling criminals have "advertised the Supreme Court's message that individuals don't have to explain themselves to the authorities and it seems unlikely that that impression can ever become widespread again."[24] In addition, certain police practices such as putting together cases solely from evidence gained through confessions seems to be dying. That the Burger Court will be willing or able to reverse the "due process revolution" and the implementing decisions of lower courts seems remote. The liberal majority of the Warren Court brought to public attention issues and tensions in the criminal justice system which needed airing. The result has been a new awareness, at least by the public elite, of the deficiencies in the system.

Reform of the criminal justice system so as to enhance the position of lower-status defendants can probably be accomplished only by increasing the adversary context of the process. This can be achieved through emphasis on professional norms, strengthening the appeals process, or financial incentives to counsel. Professionalism may not prove to be the useful value that it is in other organizations. As Feeley remarks, the low visibility of the administration of criminal justice and the low status of its clients erode the professional environment.[25] The appeals mechanism requires a convicted client with competent defense counsel. It may curb flagrant violations of due process but it is expensive, time consuming, and requires the defendant to lose at least a portion of his freedom. Financial incentives, such as those operating through the legal services programs of the Office of Economic Opportunity would seem to be one way in which counsel could be weaned away from the comfortable exchange relationships existing in so much of the system. For what appear to have been political reasons, OEO prohibited its attorneys from entering the criminal field except for very restricted purposes. Federal money now granted to the states to purchase law enforcement hardware could be more effectively spent enhancing the financial rewards of the adversaries in the system if in truth the society desires to establish justice.

The administrative practices of the legal process create for the democratic system a dilemma between the need for order and the preservation of civil liberties. As Pound noted, the most difficult problem of law is obtaining a balance "between the rules of law and magisterial discretion, which will give effect both to the general security and the individual life, with the least impairment of either. . . ."[26]

A shift in the fulcrum of this balance will result in a reallocation of the values in the system which will have political consequences for the larger society.

The view of the criminal justice system presented in this study has wide implications for an understanding of the roles played by law and politics in society. The jurisprudent's ideal of a rule of law untouched by politics seems naive when placed beside data underscoring the impact of politics on he application of law. Analysis of the legal system also accentuates the conflicting values of due process and criminal control. Perhaps as Arnold has stressed, the problem of law enforcement is to keep order while dramatizing the moral notions of the community.[27] The administration of justice exists as part of a larger political system. Its goals and processes will thus reflect the dominant values of that larger system.

NOTES

1. Earl Warren, "The Advocate and the Administration of Justice in an Urban Society," Texas Law Review, 47 (1969), 616.

2. Most important are the decisions in: *Mapp* vs. *Ohio*, 367 U.S. 643 (1961); *Gideon* vs. *Wainwright*, 372 U.S. 335 (1963); *Escobedo* vs. *Illinois*, 378 U.S. 478 (1964); *Miranda* vs. *Arizona*, 384 U.S. 436 (1966).

3. *Escobedo* vs. *Illinois*, 378 U.S. 487 (1964).

4. *Miranda* vs. *Arizona*, 384 U.S. 436 (1966).

5. *Townsend* vs. *Sain*, 372 U.S. 293 (1963).

6. Warren Burger, "State of the Federal Judiciary," delivered before the American Bar Association, St. Louis, Missouri, August 10, 1970.

7. *Mapp* vs. *Ohio*, 367 U.S. 644 (1961).

8. *Palko* vs. *Connecticut*, 302 U.S. 319 (1937).

9. Richard Harris, *Justice* (New York: Dutton, 1970).

10. Fred P. Graham, *The Self-Inflicted Wound* (New York: Macmillan, 1970).

11. Ibid., 330.

12. Burger, 3. See also: Leonard Downie, Jr., *Justice Denied* (New York: Praeger, 1971).

13. William Chambliss, *Crime and the Legal Process* (New York: McGraw-Hill, 1969), 422.

14. Roscoe Pound, *Criminal Justice in America* (New York: Holt, 1930), 212.

15. Martin Mayer, "Hogan's Office Is a Kind of Ministry of Justice," New York Times Magazine, July 23, 1967, 44.

16. Stephen L. Wasby, *The Impact of the United States Supreme Court: Some Perspectives* (Homewood, Ill.: Dorsey, 1970).

17. James P. Levine and Theodore L. Becker, "Toward and Beyond a Theory of Supreme Court Impact," paper presented at the meetings of the American Political Science Association, 1969, 2.

18. Ibid.

19. Michael Wald, Richard Ayres, David W. Hess, et al., "Interrogations in New Haven: The Impact of Miranda," Yale Law Journal, 76 (July, 1967), 1534.

20. Richard J. Medalie, Leonard Zeitz, and Paul Alexander, "Custodial Police Interrogation in Our Nation's Capital: The Attempt to Implement Miranda," Michigan Law Review, 66 (May, 1968), 1363.

21. Richard H. Seeburger and R. Stanton Wettick, Jr.,, "Miranda in Pittsburgh—A Statistical Study," University of Pittsburgh Law Review, 29 (1967), 1.

22. Levine and Becker, 9.

23. Ibid.

24. Graham, 288.

25. Malcolm M. Feeley, "Two Models of the Criminal Justice System: An Organizational Perspective," paper delivered at the 1971 annual meeting, American Political Science Association.

26. Pound, 38.

27. Thurman Arnold, "Law Enforcement—An Attempt at Social Dissection," Yale Law Journal, 42 (November, 1932), 9.

INDEX

INDEX

Adversary model: 55
Alschuler, Albert W.: 201
Arnold, Thurman: 56, 227
Assigned counsel: 169-171

Bail: 41-47
Bayley, Donald: 88
Beck, Dave: 142-143
Bell, Daniel: 22
Blau, Peter: 62
Bittner, Egon: 78
Blumberg, Abraham: 69, 177-178, 195
Bordua, David J.: 100
Bureaucracy: 51-52
Burger, Warren E.: 220-222

Carroll, Charles O.: 121, 126-130, 139-143
Chambliss, William: 71
Chevigney, Paul: 97
Chicago Jury Project: 39
Clark, Ramsey: 20, 48, 221
Clearance rate: 82-83
Combat model: 55
Counsel for indigents: 168-174
Courtroom interaction: 192-195
Cover charges: 98
Crime: amount, 22-24
Criminal bar: 161-165
Criminal control model: 52-55, 72

Dahl, Robert A.: 63
Davis, Kenneth Culp: 30

ABOUT THE AUTHOR

The influence of politics on the administration of criminal justice is the primary research concern of George F. Cole. This interest is reflected in articles in scholarly journals and an anthology, *Criminal Justice: Law and Politics.* He is currently engaged in a study of the pre-trial disposition of criminal cases and research on the impact of legal services to the poor. Dr. Cole is Associate Professor of Political Science at the University of Connecticut.